CONCILIUM

Religion in the Eighties

CONCILIUM

Concilium 156 (6/1982): Project 'X'

THE CHALLENGE OF PSYCHOLOGY TO FAITH

Edited by
Steven Kepnes
and
David Tracy

English Language Editor
Marcus Lefébure

T. & T. CLARK LTD.
Edinburgh

THE SEABURY PRESS
New York

June 1982
T. & T. Clark Ltd., 36 George Street, Edinburgh EH2 2LQ
ISBN: 0 567 30036 6

The Seabury Press, 815 Second Avenue, New York, NY 10017
ISBN: 0 8164 2387 3

Library of Congress Catalog Card No.: 81 85843

Printed in Scotland by William Blackwood & Sons Ltd., Edinburgh

Concilium: Monthly except July and August
Subscriptions 1982: UK and Rest of the World £27·00, postage and handling included; USA and Canada, all applications for subscriptions and enquiries about *Concilium* should be addressed to The Seabury Press, 815 Second Avenue, New York, NY 10017, USA.

CONTENTS

Part III
The Debate on Therapeutic Consciousness

Bulletins

Editorial: The Challenge of Psychology to Faith

THE GENERAL aim of this special issue is to illumine the challenge of different kinds of psychology to faith and the challenge of faith to psychology. The general theological model of mutually critical correlations (here between psychology and faith) has informed the editors' choice of topics. Our intent is to assure that the issue of this mutual challenge is analysed in terms of both theory and praxis.

With these basic intentions in view, the issue is divided into four sections. In section one, we have included three articles representative of major issues involved in the development of mutually critical correlations (in both theory and praxis) of contemporary psychology and religious faith. Professor Lowe's article addresses major theoretical issues as informed by the reality of suffering. Professors Browning and Siebert concentrate their attention on certain major theoretical and practical issues in the North American and European discussions of psychology and religious faith (Browning on ethics and Siebert on critical theory respectively).

In section two, the intent is to continue the discussion by focusing on five particular issues where the contemporary complexities of the inter-relationship between psychology and faith can be discerned. Again, each author has concentrated his attention on both the practical and theoretical issues at stake. The first issue of 'narrative' by Professor Kepnes shows a new and promising focus for the dialogue between psychology and theology. The second issue of 'shame' by Professor Schneider demonstrates how new psychological and theological resources can lead to a rethinking of a classic question. The next three issues remain perennial ones: first, the question of sexuality in the article by Professor Evans; second, the actual experience of therapy for believers in the article by Doctor Dominian; third, the question of the psychology of desire in Christian spirituality by Professor Moore. All five issues show how the contemporary discussion between psychology and faith remains pluralistic and promising.

Section three is organised around a single major issue in the contemporary discussion: the issue of the debate on 'therapeutic consciousness' (sometimes referred to as the debate on 'narcissism' or on the 'psychological society'). Given the central focus that this issue has provided for the contemporary discussion, the editors judged that this issue needed a multidisciplinary analysis. Hence section three is organised in four parts: first, a social-scientific analysis (in the article by Professor Doyle McCarthy); second, a social-scientific and ethical analysis (in the article by Professor Cormie); third, an analysis by a practising therapist (in the article by Doctor Dyrud); and fourth, a cultural and theological analysis (in the article by Professor Mahan). Both the importance and complexity of the contemporary debate seem well represented in the pluralistic and, in certain points, even conflictual analyses of 'therapeutic consciousness' represented in this section.

The fourth and final section remains the 'bulletins'. As always, this section is meant to be informative of more recent developments in a particular area. Assuming general knowledge of the pioneering work of Freud, Jung and Adler, we asked four experts to provide bulletins on important contemporary developments in psychology. Professor

Van Herik analyses the contemporary feminist discussion of psychology and religion; Professor Fowler summarises his own pioneering work in faith development theory; Professor Bartholomäus analyses the developments in contemporary European psychoanalytic, especially Adlerian, theory; and Professor Marie McCarthy summarises the development of family therapy in North America.

It is hoped that the pluralism of positions and methods represented in this issue will aid the continuing dialogue. For the attempt to develop mutually critical correlations in both theory and practice between psychology and faith is a major task for psychologists, therapists, pastoral counsellors, pastors, and theologians alike. If the present issue stimulates and aids that dialogue, its principal aim will have been well fulfilled. Our thanks, therefore, to all the authors for making that aim a reality.

STEVEN KEPNES, *Guest Editor*
DAVID TRACY, *Editor*

PART I

General Orientations

Walter Lowe

Psychoanalysis as an Archaeology of the History of Suffering

Here too it is true that whoso would keep his life shall lose it; but whoso shall lose it for My sake shall gain his life. Whoso means to rescue and preserve the subjective element shall lose it; but whoso gives it up for the sake of the objective, shall save it.

Karl Barth[1]

'DRIVE', 'INSTINCT', 'impulse', 'repression'. The challenge of psychology to theology would not seem far to seek. In the very language of psychoanalysis it presses itself upon us. Throughout the classic Freudian texts a bizarre vocabulary of drive and impulse, force and counterforce, evokes the fantastic image of a sort of psychic plumbing system, a sexual hydraulics of the mind! The proposal's sheer effrontery, the more offensive for being espoused in the name of science, has long drawn upon psychoanalysis the concentrated indignation of theology. For almost as long, theology's task has seemed self-evident: to grant Freud his limited truth, to refute his fundamental reductionism, and then to fish about for a more adequate psychology.

But there is another side of psychoanalysis which finds no place in this conventional critique. It has to do with the actual practice of analysis, but it is not just that analysis may be of therapeutic value. It is the fact that in its practice analysis manifests a very specific concern for the recovery of traumatic memories—for the recollection of suffering. Christian reflection, for its part, has only recently become clear about the importance of the memory of suffering for a faithful and critical theology. 'As the remembered history of suffering,' J. B. Metz observes, 'history retains the form of "dangerous tradition".'[2] Here are neglected resources for dialogue. Theology could learn more concretely the nature of such memory and means of access to it. Psychoanalysis could be instructed on the significance of its work.

It is at just this point of great promise, however, that the discussion gets derailed. For the analyst holds that the memories are not just forgotten, they have been actively *repressed*; whence it follows that to understand how they came to be repressed and how they may yet be retrieved, one must draw upon concepts of psychological force and counterforce. But that is the very language the theologians have been most anxious to expunge. For Freud, according to the common argument, was rather like Columbus. He discovered a new world, and all honour to him for that; but when he set about describing his discovery, he fell victim to certain inherited preconceptions. He imposed upon the human psyche the language of a mechanistic physics which was the paradigmatic science of his day.

The psychological challenge, on this account, is twofold and rather clear-cut—positively, to appropriate Freud's thereapeutic gains; negatively, to critique his reductionistic theory. The present essay intends to deny neither of these tasks, but only the claim to exhaustiveness. For there is a third challenge which is not so readily categorised. It concerns the psychoanalytic treatment of memory, which is closely associated with the distrusted language of force, and yet which holds great promise for theology. It concerns psychoanalysis as critical thought. To show further what this challenge is, I shall first examine some difficulties which have arisen within the traditional responses to Freud, where the critique of reductionism has tended to be the overriding concern; then, in the second half of the essay, I shall offer some constructive proposals.

1. THE ISSUE OF REDUCTIONISM

The various responses to Freud by theology, and by the humanities at large, may be surveyed in terms of a simple typology. Let us distinguish an early hermeneutical, an existentialist and a late hermeneutical response.

(*a*) Early Hermeneutical Response

This is perhaps the most straightforward position. It turns upon Wilhelm Dilthey's classic distinction between *Erklaren* and *Verstehen*, explanation and understanding. The former, which proceeds in terms of cause and effect, is the trademark of the natural sciences. But the *Geisteswissenschaften*, the human sciences, require a quite different discourse which is no less legitimate, one bearing reference to human purpose and meaning. This distinction, by which Dilthey sought to establish the human sciences on an equal footing with the natural sciences, continues to the present day in various proposals for a holistic or humanistic psychology. Now Dilthey was aware that the distinction should not be made too sharply; yet this is exactly what happened in a number of anti-reductionist arguments. Moreover, certain powerful value terms such as 'inner life' and 'meaning' tended to be located on one side of the distinction. If human meaning is the perogative of the human sciences, then by implication the natural sciences are finally meaningless. The argument is seductive, especially when not made fully explicit, but it scarcely has a holistic, integrative effect. The results are seen in the divided mind of current popular psychology, where one finds an unresolved and largely unacknowledged contradiction between the humanistic psychologies which stress the distinctively human (be it meaning, creativity or whatever) and the holistic psychologies, which hold that the modern preoccupation with human distinctiveness must give way to a participatory immersion in the body, in nature, in the universal whole.

(*b*) Existentialist Response

With the existentialists the perplexities of the earlier position become transformed into a positive and explicit programme. Meaning and purpose are unambiguously placed to one side of the human equation. To the other side lies scientific casual explanation, which may distract us from the human reality: it is secondary at best, and often suspect. For the Sartre of *Being and Nothingness*, the Freudian psychology amounts to a wilful self-delusion, an exercise in bad faith. But the problem cast out the front door by a radical clarification returns quietly through the back. For in much of existentialism it is argued that human existence is constituted by a fundamental paradox, namely the fact that we are both finite and free. To neglect *either* pole, transcendence *or* facticity, cuts the nerve of our very existence; it entails a self-delusion which some theologians have equated with sin. And yet, this caution notwithstanding, there is in existentialism, as in the earlier position, an undeniable tendency to place the value terms to one side of the crucial distinction. It is no accident that existentialism is known specifically as a philosophy of freedom; for it is freedom the position asserts, in the face of all who would deny or reduce it. Thus the importance attached to the openness of the future as opposed to the fixity of the past, the realm of facticity. This unstinting advocacy of freedom is meant to critique the scientific reductionist; yet in the end it bids fair to be reductionist itself, reductionist in the opposite direction, as it were, in light of the existentialist's own more considered pronouncements about irreducible polarity. One may wonder whether Freud may not have something to say which the existentialists ought in principle to have recognised, but which in fact is lost in the existential psychology.[3]

(*c*) Late Hermeneutical Response

This question brings us to the late hermeneutical position, which we shall consider at somewhat greater length. Like the existentialists, Paul Ricoeur undertakes a philosophy of the human subject. But existentialism tends to make appeal to introspective intuition, a procedure which, on Ricoeur's view, risks a narcissistic self-absorption. Thus Ricoeur prefers to approach the human subject *in*directly, by way of the cultural texts in which subjectivity has been objectified. The return to hermeneutics is prompted, in other words, by a desire to purify our fallible self-understanding. Hermeneutics becomes a means toward a critical comprehension of the self.

But if it is true of hermeneutics in general that the objectivity of the texts is a way of getting us outside ourselves, then might not the same be true *a fortiori* of the study of a text such as Freud's, which is so very resistant to our common sense? Might not there be something even in Freud's mechanistic metaphors which bears the seeds not of an alien objectivism, but of a liberating objectivity? That is the wager which undergirds Ricoeur's massive study of Freud. Ricoeur says of Freud's peculiar vocabulary, which mixes with such abandon the two types of discourse which Dilthey so assiduously distinguished: 'I hope to show that there are good reasons for this apparent ambiguity, that this mixed discourse is the *raison d'être* of psychoanalysis.'[4] This proposal marks a fundamental advance. It suggests, in a manner not previously possible, that Freud's language is not simply a product of confusion, a category mistake, but that it represents a positive achievement which must be confronted and worked through. The implication is that it would be misguided to conceive of the Freudian legacy solely in reductionist terms, i.e., as consisting solely of the language of force; and that it would be *equally* distorting to translate Freud exhaustively into *revisionist* terms, i.e., into the language of meaning.

Ricoeur supports his premiss by noting that the realm in which psychoanalysis operates is at language's remote lower boundary, where inchoate desire struggles to gain expression. 'What makes desire the limit concept at the frontier between the organic and the psychical is the fact that desire is both the nonspoken and the wish-to-speak [i.e., the meaning, "le vouloir-dire"], the unnameable and the potency to speak.'[5] Thus Freud's anomalous language may perhaps be justified in that it corresponds, in some still ill-defined way, to the boundary at which the analyst works.

For us mortals, living within language as we do, that boundary is a sort of horizon. It is a limit; and because a limit, it is the place where illusion most readily appears. We imagine that this or that desired object may be the realisation of all our dreams. We confuse object and horizon, the instance and the desire; it is a sort of idolatry. The task of therapy, in effect, is to recover the distinction between the two, relativising the object against the limitless horizon, the ever-receding expanse. There is to therapy, then, this perpetual, critical task of learning to live with limits, including the limits imposed by the very boundlessness of desire.

But there is, Ricoeur goes on to say, an upper horizon as well. For just as our language is rooted in desire, it is simultaneously able to transcend itself in the direction of ideal sense. This is the direction attested by Hegel; and Ricoeur displays great subtlety in arguing for an irreducible dialectic or interplay between the Freudian archaeology and the Hegelian teleology. As his study draws to a close, however, there emerges a *second*, larger sense of 'teleology' which gathers up both archaeology and the earlier teleology. That this is not the advance it might seem is evident in the very notion of horizon, which declines from being possibility-and-limit to being primarily possibility, to the detriment of its role as critical limit. And if, disturbed by this turn of events, one then returns to Ricoeur's textual analysis of Freud, one finds the vast preponderance of argument is devoted to showing that the language of force never appears in isolation, but is always related to the language of meaning. Almost entirely lacking is any equally emphatic exposition as to why the language of force is there in the first place, or why it should be retained.[6]

(*d*) A Preliminary Assessment

We may conclude that while it has contributed much, the late hermeneutical position finally succumbs to a difficulty analogous to that observed in the previous two. Again certain distinctions have been made, again the integrity of each side has been affirmed: on one level, the significance of the two languages; on another level, the mutual irreducibility of archaeology and teleology. And yet again a premium has been placed on one side to the detriment of the other; indeed to the detriment of the entire dialectic.

How is one to account for this recurrent bias, this pattern of diminishment, in even the most discerning responses to Freud? Theodor Adorno provides a clue when he cautions that 'in the history of philosophy we repeatedly find epistemological categories turned into moral ones'.[7] That is precisely the turn that is taken, to a greater or lesser extent, in each of the foregoing positions. The transformation has the effect of underlining the discussion's human significance, but there is an unintended side effect as well. For once the discussion is cast in moral terms, it becomes increasingly difficult for the 'lower' categories, such as the language of force or the archaeology, to compete with the 'higher' for their fair share of that significance. Moreover, when the moral note is stressed, as it commonly is when the critique of reductionism becomes the overriding concern, it may readily seem that the 'higher' is in need of protection—and that it is the 'lower' itself which poses the threat. The result is an imbalance, a skewing of the ongoing discussion, which makes itself felt in even so judicious a treatment as the Ricoeurian hermeneutic.

Yet to return to a neat separation of the moral and the epistemological is not a possibility; for reductionism does require attention and moral issues are indeed at stake. The way forward is to insist that if moral significance is to be ascribed to the one set of terms, then it must be ascribed with equal seriousness to the other set as well. And that is the question before us—can we discern an inherent moral significance in the archaeology, and in the language of force?

2. THE ARCHAEOLOGY OF SUFFERING

From time to time when I visit the local bookstore, I pace off the six-tiered section of shelves devoted to popular psychology, transpersonal psychology, parapsychology, astrology of personality, self-help and self-improvement. Recently it has been running around thirty-four feet. This seemingly endless stream of literature is reflective of the fact that middle-class American culture, and the middle-class church along with it, has for years been awash in a vague but congenial optimism about the vistas of human potential. This sense of limitless possibility is sponsored by a sort of psychology; and whatever that psychology is, it is *not* reductionistic—not in the usual sense of the word. It affirms religion, it affirms the human; there is little it will not affirm. But what it affirms, it swallows up, while itself remaining formless. It is lacking in the prophetic, it is lacking in the critical. It is, to adapt a phrase from T. E. Hulme, psychology as spilt religion.

One reason this thing has become so rampant is that it has caught us on our theological blind side. One can of course object that in certain of its procedures it tries to manipulate God; but the various disciples will readily respond: 'Oh no, we are *against* manipulation!' Beyond that modest exchange, the traditional theological response seems to have little resource with which to mount a critique of this amiable psychology. It becomes apparent, in restrospect, that we have laboured to construct a theological Maginot line. Our conceptual artillery, fixed as it was in the direction of the reductionists, was incapable of readjusting when a different psychology swept upon us from another direction. And soon it no longer mattered; the Church's critical faculties had been overwhelmed in a warm, viscous flood of affirmation.

I exaggerate a little, perhaps, but only to draw attention to a very real phenomenon. It is the cultural embodiment of the conceptual bias which was traced in the previous section. It makes palpable the need for a more evenhanded approach: one which can grasp the critical import of the very aspect of psychoanalysis most readily dismissed by the anti-reductionist argument, and by the popular psychologies.

(*a*) The Language of Force

Nothing is more central to the practice of analysis than the phenomenon of transference, the powerful interpersonal relationship generated between client and therapist which provides the crucial leverage for dealing with the client's resistances. It is a matter of debate the extent to which the relationship requires of the therapist an empathetic response to the client's needs. But there is agreement that, whatever else, the therapist must maintain a considerable measure of detachment. The therapist must never cease to regard the dynamics of transference with a canny, analytic eye; for he or she is constantly drawing upon the interpersonal dynamic, channelling it in such a way as to further the emergent therapeutic goal. But this is in effect to say that the therapist *uses* the relationship: the therapist treats the I-Thou as an It!

What could possibly justify such a procedure? Either it is grounds for rejecting psychoanalysis out of hand—or it is evidence of how serious the problem is. On the latter premiss, the tactical objectification which occurs in analytic practice may be viewed as a measure necessitated by a certain objectification, a certain reification, which has occurred within the individual. The human past may be conceived as the cumulative result of a constant process of sedimentation. Where there has been pain, the very memory may harden and contract, like a scar forming over a wound. The injury is then borne into the present in the form of certain patterns of behaviour such as obsession or hysteria. But whatever the form it may have taken, there is to such injury a common, identifying trait: that the individual has become less free, more constrained—in a real sense, more mechanical.

But might this phenomenon not be related, then, to Freud's mechanistic language? Much of the language, no doubt, is simply meant to be naturalistic and must be accepted or rejected as such. But might it not also refer in part to *second* nature: that is, to the acquired but long-established set of habits and mannerisms, quirks and vulnerabilities, which are ingrained in one's character? In that case the reference would not simply be to some ultimate substrate of animality, the source of unreflective impulse, but to the *interaction* of impulse, decision and circumstance, and to the complex layering which results—in short, to the individual *histories* which make us what we are.[8]

(*b*) Discerning the Challenges

This interpretation of Freud has definite anti-reductionist implications, which become clear the moment one stresses, as we have done, that even his most mechanistic language refers not simply to some isolated instinctual nature, but also to history. One may draw the conclusion that even at his most deterministic, Freud tacitly acknowledged the role of human freedom. The argument would be much like Ricoeur's, when he shows that the language of force is never entirely detached from a correlative language of sense.

But stressing the note of freedom diverts attention from one decisive fact, namely that we are dealing not with history in some generalised sense, but quite specifically with the history *of suffering*. It further obscures the fact, which has already been sufficiently obscured, that this is a history which has been assiduously denied, impacted and forgotten; and that often all we have left by which to recover it are the omissions and tics, the distortions and scars—precisely the marks of *un*freedom—which that history has bequeathed us.

Now if this distinctive face of psychoanalysis does pose its own distinctive challenge to theology—a challenge of theodicy, a challenge to keep faith with the history of suffering as it presents itself in this humble psychological guise—it is not a challenge which can be ranged unreflectively alongside the previous two. For there exists between the present concern and the previously recognised tasks of appropriating therapeutic benefit and critiquing reductionist theory, a substantial conceptual tension. Thus in the case just noted, the anti-reductionist preoccupation with the reality of freedom inevitably diverted attention from the archaeological effort to patiently, methodically bring to light the intricate network of human caughtness.

The point may be put more emphatically. It must be said that a true word spoken in the wrong circumstances becomes functionally untrue. It becomes a means of denial, a form of ideology. To maintain contra a psychological determinism that the human person is possessed of freedom is undoubtedly fitting and true. And telling an individual that she is free to choose may be for that person, at a difficult moment in her life, a gesture of trust and assurance. But the very same words spoken at another moment may evince a bland insensitivity to what the person is, at that moment, going through. And spoken in the abstract, it may come as an empty truth which mocks the reality—much as the formally accurate statement that all persons in a certain society enjoy equal rights may gloss over the fact that some happen to exercise those rights from positions of economic privilege while others are acutely disadvantaged.

The challenges are multiple, then. And to know which is real at which moment requires the unceasing exercise of a concrete and compassionate discernment.

(*c*) The Real Reductionism

How then are we to discern the present challenge to theology? I shall offer just a few remarks in closing. The common critique has rightly perceived that more is at stake in Freud than the fate of a particular theory. Psychoanalysis is a movement and an institution; it impacts upon our culture. And in so far as it propounds a diminished image of the self, it contributes to the creation of a one-dimensional society.

Now regarding contemporary culture, Victor Preller has made an astute observation. 'In the modern world,' he writes, '. . . a basic source of anxiety is the underlying suspicion and fear that the mind of man has in fact exhausted the nature of the real. To prove that it does not—to hold out the logical possibility of a God who might care—is tantamount to psychological salvation.'[9] The remark takes reductionism seriously, to the point of recognising that our very sense of reality has been affected. Further, it helps one understand why the popular psychological movements should have struck such a responsive chord despite their lack of critical depth. Because of the underlying anxiety that the one-dimensional world of a controlling technology may in fact be all there is, the most meagre suggestion to the contrary, even a mysticism of jogging, may be *felt as* a subjective, experiential liberation.

But there is a fundamental danger here. In a situation where there is such urgent need for any glimmering of transcendence, the theological task gets shortcircuited. Theology becomes the errand boy of affirmation. It must be said, therefore, that precisely *because* the ravages of reductionism are so all-pervasive, the threat cannot be met head on. We cannot simply settle—as we are pressed by the urgency of the task to settle—for carving out a little space for subjectivity, a little space for freedom and transcendence. For it is just such compartmentalisation of the realm of freedom to one side, the realm of determinism to the other—the language of poetry to one side, the language of fact to the other—which creates the one-dimensional world.

The phenomenon of human diminishment is all too real and we ourselves, in our very forms of thought, are not exempt from it. For that very reason the matter cannot be addressed by *ad hoc* measures or alliances of convenience. Indeed, in the end it must be addressed by nothing less than the entirety of the Christian story, from creation through redemption. The challenge of psychology to theology is finally the challenge for theology to be itself—in all its positive fullness, in all its critical power.

Notes

1. *Dogmatics in Outline* (New York 1959) p. 16.
2. *Faith in History and Society* (New York 1980) p. 110.
3. A fuller discussion would treat the manner in which a more complex figure such as Heidegger may transcend this paradigm.
4. *Freud and Philosophy* (New Haven/London 1970) p. 65.
5. *Ibid*. p. 457.
6. For an analogous critique of Jurgen Habermas, the other major representative of the late hermeneutical position, see Russell Keat *The Politics of Social Theory* (Chicago/Oxford 1981).
7. *Negative Dialectics* (New York 1973) p. 35.
8. See Russell Jacoby *Social Amnesia* (Boston 1975), pp. 4, 31, 65. Despite its polemical character, or perhaps because of it, Jacoby's work is a rich source of critical insight. The present argument, like much else in the present essay, is treated at greater length in Walter Lowe *Evil and the Unconscious*, to be published by Scholars Press (Chico, California).
9. *Divine Science and the Science of God* (Princeton 1967) p. 31.

Don Browning

The Estrangement of Pastoral Care from Ethics

1. THE ISSUE: THE ESTRANGEMENT OF PASTORAL CARE FROM ETHICS

PASTORAL CARE and counselling in North American churches, both Protestant and Catholic, has been shaped in recent decades by two inter-related cultural trends—the growing influence of the secular psychologies and the increased autonomy of all helping disciplines from moral philosophy and moral theology. As psychiatry, social work, and all the psychotherapies have depended upon the modern psychologies—whether it be psychoanalysis, Jungianism, humanistic psychology, or some form of behaviourism—so has North American pastoral care and counselling increasingly relied upon these resources. In addition, just as the helping disciplines such as psychiatry and social work have grown increasingly autonomous from any grounding in moral philosophy, so has pastoral care and counselling in recent decades become increasingly independent of moral theology or theological ethics.

Several reasons can be cited to explain the changes which the Church, particularly the mainline Protestant Churches and to some extent the Catholic Church as well, has undergone. The most powerful single explanation is sociological. The increasing pluralism of modern societies and the multiplication and atomisation of 'plausibility structures', in Peter Berger's sense of that phrase, have made it increasingly difficult for any of our major institutions, and especially the Church, to sustain a convincing and widely accepted coherent perspective on personal morality and values.[1] One way the Church has coped with its own weakened capacity to direct lives is to shift its emphasis. Except in more conservative circles, the Church now primarily seeks to maintain warm relations, communicate acceptance and support, and help confused, depressed, or otherwise broken people regain some initiative and control without paying too much attention to the specific moral or spiritual direction of their lives.

Second, the Church's pastoral care and counselling has been influenced profoundly by a diagnostic bias widely held by much of contemporary psychological and psychotherapeutic theory. This bias is that moralism is *a* major cause, if not *the* major cause, of mental health difficulties in modern societies. Moralism is variously defined, but it primarily seems to mean making arbitrary, premature, or poorly timed moral appeals which repress or harshly suppress normal human impulses, interests, or needs. Freud's 'rigid superego', Jung's 'persona', Rogers's 'conditions of worth', and Sullivan's 'rigid self-system' are all variations on this theme. All of this has led modern psychology to distrust not only blind superego dictates in particular, but in general moral philosophy, moral theology, and in fact, formal ethics of all kinds.

This further has led to what Steward Hiltner has called an 'eductive' approach to care and counselling, whereby ministers and pastoral counsellors have tried to help people by letting the troubled person bring her or his own moral and non-moral value framework to the counselling situation.[2] This stance has had the genuine merit of giving troubled persons a non-threatening environment in which to cope with their problems and of keeping the Church and minister in contact with people without taking too much responsibility for the actual moral content of their lives.

Indeed, there is little doubt that both Catholic and Protestant care and counselling had problems with moralism in the first half of the twentieth century, and to some extent still do. The rigid and deductive character of the Catholic moral theology manuals is now widely acknowledged. The moralistic character of the Protestant ethic also has been well exposed. But the excesses and deficiencies of a moral tradition at particular moments in history should not be exaggerated into more generalised arguments for the necessary moral neutrality of helping relationships under all circumstances and should not be used as a pretext for continuing the present estrangement between the Church's care and counselling and moral theology and theological ethics.

The alternative, however, is to relate, once again, the practices of pastoral care and counselling to moral theology and theological ethics but to do this in such a way as to avoid the excesses of the older moralism and to preserve the actual gains which have occurred because of the introduction into our helping professions, both religious and secular, of psychological and dynamic points of view. For indeed, real gains have been made. I will mention three of these advances which it would be a tragedy to lose.

First, we have learned from the secular psychologies the importance, in all forms of helping people, of temporary suspensions of moral judgment. The first step in helping another person is establishing a relationship of trust. Premature exercise of moral judgments invariably inhibits the development of trusting relationships. But the temporary and heuristic suspension of moral judgments should not be confused with the wider elimination of any moral context whatsoever from our acts of care and counselling.

Second, we have also learned from the contemporary psychologies the way our freedom is conditioned by our developmental histories. When the psychologies, especially psychoanalytic psychology, are provided the proper philosophical base, they do not in reality teach the total determinism of the human will. Rather, they depict the human will as thick or heavy, to use a concept of Paul Ricoeur.[3] Our will or agency is a conditioned will, conditioned by the unique history of the biological and social forces which shape each individual. The secular psychologies have given us important tools for the analysis and understanding of the heaviness or conditionedness of the human will. Hence, the modern psychologies, when rightly understood, are instruments for the enhancement of human freedom. By helping us understand the forces that limit freedom, they enable us to maximise more accurately and insightfully the actual exercise of freedom.

Third, the contemporary psychologies, especially the depth psychologies, have shown the dialectical relation between the 'high' and 'low' in human nature and motivation.[4] By these metaphors, I intend to refer respectively to those structures related to reason, morality, imagination (the high) and instinct, need, and passion (the low). The basic thrust of the depth psychologies (the later Freud, Jung, Heinz Hartmann, Erik Erikson, and the more recent object-relations school) is to suggest that certain higher adaptive processes associated with cognition, intelligence, generalisation, and morality do not function well without receiving data from the lower order adaptive processes connected with instinctive tendencies and certain interpersonal or object-relational lines of development, some of which are formed quite early in life.[5]

This is the wisdom of the therapeutic emphasis upon 'feeling our feelings'. Our feelings do not in themselves tell us the nature of either the morally good or the true. But our feelings give us food for thought; they inform reflective processes.

Hence, our contemporary psychologies have bequeathed significant learnings which must not be lost as we attempt once again to bring our practical therapies in contact with ethics. In my book *The Moral Context of Pastoral Care* (1976) and more recently in *Pluralism and Personality: William James and Some Contemporary Cultures of Psychology* (1980), I took some tentative steps towards overcoming the estrangement which has developed between care and counselling, both secular and religious, and ethics.[6] In *The Moral Context of Pastoral Care*, I argued that not only should there be a moral context to all forms of care and counselling, both religious and secular, but, in addition, this context should be grounded in practical moral rationality. I argued, in fact, that the Christian religion, with its close association on the one hand with the practical moral rationality of midrashic and rabbinic Judaism and on the other with Platonic and Stoic moral rationality, actually gave some sacred legitimation to the use of moral rationality in developing its ethics.[7] Of course, it always has been acknowledged by the Catholic moral theology tradition that there was a place in religious ethics for natural human moral rationality as well as divine revelation, and that when both are properly perceived and interpreted there would be a genuine correlation between them. Protestant ethics, on the other hand, has been far less willing to admit a role for practical moral rationality and has generally tried to anchor its ethics in some kind of dentological divine command theory of either a rule or act variety.[8] Theoretically, then, traditional Protestant ethics should lend itself to moralism more easily than should Catholic ethics. Catholic ethics, more than traditional Protestant ethics, should be able to provide reasons for its moral positions which should have some convincingness in themselves.[9] Although a reasoned ethic should escape some of the pitfalls of moralism better than a more strictly divine command perspective, it still can fall into moralism if it overlooks some of the issues of timing, developmental history, psychological readiness, and capacity for freedom.

I propose, then, a new intellectual effort to overcome the estrangement of theological ethics and pastoral care and counselling. This effort would attempt to relate a rationally and critically articulate theological ethic with dynamic psychology. Such a programme would be distinguishable immediately from the call for a closer relation between psychiatry and ethics to be found in the work of Hobart Mowrer, William Glasser and John Drakeford.[10] Their lack of interest in a critical ethic distinguishes their programme from mine. On the other hand, my proposal is also different from a simple pre-Freudian return to a strictly moral theology or theological-ethical point of view. I propose a return to ethics after passing through the detour of dynamic psychology's heightened awareness of the concrete needs and actual stages of empirical human development. I propose a return to an ethic to govern all forms of care and counselling, but one informed more completely by what Paul Ricoeur calls an 'archaeology of the subject'.[11]

But how can a theological-ethical perspective on the person take account of psychological dynamics without losing the integrity of the normative point of view? In the remaining pages of this essay, I want to attempt to answer this question. In doing so I will be setting forth a theory of practical moral rationality which might help establish the moral context of pastoral care and counselling. This is something I called for in *The Moral Context of Pastoral Care*, but have had to wait until recently to actually work out.[12]

2. A RESPONSE: A THEORY OF PRACTICAL MORAL RATIONALITY

The following constitutes a brief outline of a *revised correlational theory of practical* moral rationality. By revised correlational method, I mean to refer to the meaning of that approach to theology as it has been developed in the theology of David Tracy and others. Here I apply it to the field of religious ethics and develop it in ways unique to my own theological programme. In general, the revised correlational programme attempts to correlate critically both the questions and answers derived from various interpretations of the central testimony of the Christian witness with the questions and answers implicit in various interpretations of ordinary human experience. The same method in theological ethics means a critical correlation between the norms for human action and fulfilment revealed in various interpretations of the Christian tradition and the norms implicit in various interpretations of ordinary human experience. To say that this correlation task is to be critical is to say it should be basically public and philosophical. It should attempt to bring faith to the intelligibility of reason and public discourse.

In what follows below I will set out briefly my understanding of the five levels of practical moral rationality. I will then suggest some ways dynamic psychology can relate to these levels and do so in such a way as to overcome the estrangement between theological ethics and pastoral care and counselling.

(*a*) The five levels of practical moral rationality

There are *five levels of practical moral rationality*: (1) a metaphorical level, (2) an obligational level, (3) a need-value level, (4) a predictive-contextual level, and (5) a rule-role level. The task of moral theology or theological ethics is first to do a hermeneutics of the implications of the Christian fact for these five levels and then critically correlate the results of this exercise with an interpretation of the implications for these levels of various interpretations of ordinary or secular experience.

The *metaphorical level* of moral thinking is indeed the most fundamental. But, at the same time, it does not determine the details of the other levels. The metaphorical level seeks to answer such questions as: what is the nature of the ultimate (in the sense of most determinative) context of experience and what influence does it have on our moral action? To answer these questions, one necessarily resorts to metaphorical thinking. We never have tangible sensory experiences of this ultimate context and to refer to it at all, we must resort to metaphorical and symbolic language. Our more discrete moral decisions never take place in a vacuum; they also occur in a larger context which we interpret through metaphors as to whether we experience it as a whole as warm or cold, indifferent or responsive, predictable or capricious. To convey our full apprehension of this ultimate context, we often must resort to stories which give our root metaphors a narrative and dramatic structure. Metaphors such as God is 'love' or the world is 'redeemable' influence our theories of obligation, but they do not determine them in all respects. Basically, they help us discern, appreciate, and value life and the world in certain ways. This, in turn, helps to answer whether life is meaningful and whether moral action within it is possible and worthwhile.

One does not arrive at the more directly *obligational level* of moral rationality until one discovers more specific propositions which enunciate moral maxims. One has arrived at the obligational level of moral rationality when one chooses a statement that one believes summarises what it means to be moral, such as Kant's categorical imperative which says 'Act only on that maxim which you can at the same time will to be a universal law'. The Golden Rule and the second Great Commandment ('You shall love your neighbour as yourself') are also statements of moral obligation. As I indicated above, different metaphorical representations of the ultimate context of reality can be associated with different theories of obligation; our metaphors of ultimacy influence but do not necessarily dictate our principles of moral obligation. For instance, Kant's categorical imperative can be placed within a Buddhist, existentialist or Christian understanding of ultimate reality. On the other hand, one's overall understanding of how Kant's principle would actually operate—whether, for instance, it would entail any interest in the claims of future generations—would clearly be seen differently, depending upon the set of metaphors used by a particular community.

The most powerful single principle of obligation, in my opinion, is associated with the Kantian categorical imperative and its powerful restatement in John Rawl's principle of impartiality. Recently, this tradition has been forcefully introduced into religious ethics by Ronald Green in his book entitled *Religious Reason*.[13] It is basically a deontological principle in the strict meaning of that word, i.e., it does not arrive at its understanding of the right or morally obligatory with reference to that act or acts which will produce the largest amount of good over evil, as do the teleologists.[14] Rather it asks what is just or fair when the parties involved in a decision are impartial or blind to the particular benefits a decision might yield to them. It is a principle close, if not identical, to the basic meaning of the Golden Rule and the principle of neighbour love, as Green and others have pointed out.[15]

I quickly will state what I mean by the other three levels of moral rationality before I return and illustrate the way dynamic psychology can relate to this theory of ethics. Although this Kant-Rawl's principle of obligation is superior over other more teleological principles such as ethical egoist or utilitarian views, it really cannot be fully implemented without some reference to a theory of *nonmoral needs, goods, and values*. What are the basic human needs and interests—such as food, water, sex, affiliation, identity, safety, self-actualisation, generativity, etc.—which are deserving of just and impartial distribution? This is the third level of moral rationality—the so-called *need-value* level. It is at this level that psychology, in its study of human motivation and need, can make a direct and indispensable contribution to ethics, even religious ethics. But psychology is not the only discipline that can do this; biology, especially sociobiology, can help us identify fundamental human needs and tendencies. The ethical point of view does not say that all tendencies and needs are good and therefore should be actualised; but even Rawl's principle of justice as fairness requires, finally, some theory of our central tendencies so that just decisions can be made about which of them can be fairly and harmoniously organised together.

Finally, our human needs, even if they are to be fairly and impartially provided for, must be accommodated in particular situations and particular environments which always place additional constraints on which goods can be justly organised together. This is why moral rationality requires disciplines which help interpret the possibilities of various *contexts* and which *predict* the likely outcomes of specific lines of action. Psychology is one among many empirically-oriented disciplines that can help theological ethics with this level of moral rationality. This level of moral rationality, the fourth, is the *contextual-predictive level*. The fifth and last level is what I call the *rule-role level*. When we have gone through the four prior levels of judgment, we finally engender specific rules governing our actions in particular situations and specific roles which we occupy (which are themselves governed by rules) in the social systems which organise our lives. Psychology can play a role at this level as well, for psychology with its theories of human needs, motivations, and central tendencies helps us to understand which needs are being served and which are being sacrificed by the various rules and roles which guide and bind our lives.

(*b*) The way dynamic psychology can relate to these levels

In conclusion, psychology can relate to this view of moral rationality in two ways: (i) it can help make applicational judgments about where people are, their readiness to grasp and live by a certain moral point of view, and about the psychological blocks and impediments which inhibit them from growing into a fully comfortable owning of certain moral expectations, and (ii) it can inform substantially level three, the need-value level, by helping us determine the nature and hierarchy of our central tendencies and needs. The first or applicational view of the relation of psychology to ethics primarily helps inform the process of relating our moral rationality to various situations and various people who are at different developmental levels. The second method makes psychological information (or at least intuitive judgments which lead to the same insights) indispensable to the substantive heart of moral reflection.

The first applicational or processive way of relating psychology to theological ethics goes far in overcoming moralism. For instance, it is possible to do a psychological analysis of the effects of several of the five levels I outlined and through this discern how individuals are able to cope with various moral claims. For example, we can study the psychological effects of different metaphors of ultimacy and determine how they support or inhibit people's capacity to act. William James studied mechanistic, monistic, mystical, and theistic metaphors this way, attempting to discern psychologically whether they tended to inspire a sense of personal agency—the sense that one lives in a world where free and responsible action is possible. It was James's judgment that monistic metaphors have the psychological results of suggesting security but not an enhanced sense of agency, that mechanistic metaphors inspire neither security nor freedom, that theistic metaphors inspire a limited sense of security but a greatly heightened sense of agency and responsibility, and that mystical metaphors are ambiguous depending upon whether they are interpreted monistically or theistically.[16]

Psychoanalytic psychology of religion, especially the recent work of Rizzutto, is very potent in its capacity to discern the idiosyncratic meaning to individuals of such symbols as father, mother, or love as they might be applied to God.[17] Of course, these psychological analyses of the effect of various religious metaphors do not prove either their rightness or wrongness, but they do give us a heightened awareness of the psychological meanings of our metaphors. Awareness of this helps us overcome moralism; it makes us more sensitive and accurate in our communication and more tolerant of the range of misunderstandings and the reasons for them. This is relevant for the Church's communication in general, and it is certainly important for communication within any context, religious or secular, of care and counselling.

But an even clearer case for the applicational role of psychology can be found at the obligational level. For example, the research of Lawrence Kohlberg has helped chart the stages of moral development. He has discovered six stages of moral development, with the highest stage exhibiting the features of the Kant-Rawl's understanding of universal impartiality discussed above.[18] He finds these stages, as follows, to be invariant and structurally definable: a punishment stage, an instrumental-hedonistic stage, an interpersonal concordance or 'good-boy—good-girl' stage, a law and order stage, a contractual stage, and finally a universalistic stage. But the greatest point of Kohlberg's discoveries, from the standpoint of this article, is his contention that people at lower levels of moral judgment can grow only if moral appeals are made just slightly above the level at which they are functioning; stage two people may be able to understand appeals presented on stage three reasoning, but probably not those made from stage five and six. This has obvious implications for inducing moral development. To confront children and adults at lower stages of moral development with unqualified universalistic demands may be the height of moralism. This is not to say that we do not want people to grow toward more universalistic moral judgments, but in order to do this we may need to bracket these claims temporarily and confront them with claims nearer their level of comprehension. Much of what happens in psychotherapy is just this. Gene Abroms has argued that psychotherapy is not neutral; rather, it uses dynamic insight to mitigate conflict and free the client to make better use of appeals made by the therapist from stages of moral reasoning only slightly above where the client is in his or her own moral thinking. Such precision may help overcome moralism, but it does not make psychotherapy any less a moral process.[19]

Time and space do not allow me to carry forward in detail this discussion of the applicational relevance of psychology to the other three stages of moral rationality. I have touched already on psychology's role with regard to levels three and four in the discussion above, i.e., in analysing contexts and making predictions and its task in analysing the specific psychological effects of different rules and roles.

What is more important, however, than the applicational role of psychology in helping to overcome moralism is the more substantive way psychology can inform level three. Psychology helps tabulate and assess our central needs and our central human tendencies. Not all of our human tendencies are central; some are relatively unimportant wants or wishes. And, indeed, some of our more central ones are not always easily reconcilable, such as the need for security, on the one hand, and independence, on the other. Human needs and tendencies are neither moral nor immoral in themselves. But it is precisely the task of ethics justly and impartially to actualise and harmonise human needs and tendencies. To do this, some are curtailed, some are suppressed, and some are organised in certain ways in order not to jeopardise and destroy others. When theological ethics is seen to be in the service of human needs, as I dare say it was at least supposed to have been in the Catholic tradition, it is far less likely to be perceived as moralistic. Because of what psychology can contribute to judgment at level three, it can make a contribution to overcoming the tendency toward moralism in moral theology and theological ethics. The future of pastoral care and counselling, in both Catholic and Protestant circles, in North American and elsewhere, must be found in new intellectual efforts to overcome the present estrangement between religious ethics and the psychotherapeutic psychologies. And this dictum, I believe, is equally relevant to all so-called forms of secular care and counselling, wherever they exist.

Notes

1. Peter Berger *The Sacred Canopy* (New York 1967) pp. 126-153.
2. Seward Hiltner *Preface to Pastoral Theology* (Nashville 1958) pp. 151-161.
3. Paul Ricoeur *The Symbolism of Evil* (New York 1967) pp. 335-345.
4. For a development of this idea of 'high' and 'low', see Don Browning, *Generative Man: Psychoanalytic Perspective* (New York 1975) p. 147.
5. It is my conviction that Heinz Hartmann states this truth most successfully in his *Ego Psychology and the Problem of Adaptation* (New York 1958) pp. 74-79.
6. Don Browning *The Moral Context of Pastoral Care* (Philadelphia 1976); *Pluralism and Personality: William James and Some Contemporary Cultures of Psychology* (Lewisburg 1980).
7. *The Moral Context of Pastoral Care* pp. 46, 91-115.
8. For a discussion of some of the differences between Protestant and Catholic ethics, see James Gustafson *Protestant and Catholic Ethics* (Chicago 1978).
9. *Ibid.* pp. 30-59.
10. O. Hobart Mowrer *The Crisis in Psychiatry and Religion* (New York 1961) and *The New Group Therapy* (New York 1964); William Glasser *Reality Therapy* (New York 1965); John Drakeford *Integrity Therapy* (Nashville 1967).
11. Paul Ricoeur *Freud and Philosophy* (New Haven 1970) p. 439.

12. For a more complete statement of what follows, see my article entitled 'Psychology as Religio-Ethical Thinking' forthcoming, and my forthcoming book entitled *Religious Ethics and Pastoral Care* (1983).

13. Ronald Green *Religious Reason* (New York 1978).

14. William Frankena *Ethics* (Englewood Cliffs 1973) pp. 14-16.

15. Green *Religious Reason* pp. 130-131.

16. For a fuller review of James's critical psychology of religion of these metaphors, see my 'William James's Philosophy of Mysticism' *Journal of Religion* (January 1979) 56-70, and my *Pluralism and Personality* pp. 237-267.

17. Ava-Maria Rizzuto *The Birth of the Living God* (Chicago 1979).

18. Lawrence Kohlberg *The Philosophy of Moral Development* (New York 1971).

19. Gene Abroms 'The Place of Values in Psychotherapy' *Journal of Marriage and Family Counseling* (October 1978) 3-17.

Rudolf Siebert

Religion and Psychoanalysis: European Situation

IN EUROPE today, pro- as well as anti-religious psychoanalysts can be found. There are psychoanalysts in different European countries, who are practising Jews or Christians, as well as others who consider the interest in religion a symptom of unsolved problems between ego and superego, ego and id, ego and environment. The position taken in this essay on the relationship between religious faith and secular psychoanalysis differs from both types of psychoanalysts and is representative of a third group of philosophical psychoanalysts in Europe: the critical theorists of the *Institute for Social Research* in Frankfurt am Main, Germany. The critical theorists most informed by and concerned with religion as well as with psychoanalysis are M. Horkheimer, W. Benjamin, Th. W. Adorno, H. Marcuse and E. Fromm and their friends and disciples.[1]

The critical theorists differentiate sharply between religious thought concepts and the human experience behind it. For the religious person, no matter if he is a believer in religious dogmas or not, life is a problem. It is characterised by fundamental contradictions. The very fact of having been born and having to suffer and to die is a riddle. A riddle which is to be answered not only in thought, but in the whole way of life, not only in theory, but also in practice. Life is not something simply positivistically and accidentally given, and as such acquiring no further meaning than to eat, drink, survive, procreate, have pleasure and take part in events according to some ethical norm. Sex, car and career, the symbols of much of life in European advanced capitalistic society, do not grant sufficient meaning. The religious individual senses painfully the profound existential antagonism of life between freedom and necessity, unity and separation, knowledge and ignorance, subject and object. His/her efforts are directed toward finding the absolute solution to these contradictions: reconciliation, justification, happiness, redemption. There is no goal in the life of the *homo religiosus* which is not subordinated to this very attempt of a complete solution. Here lies in fact the Kierkegaardian difference between the aesthetical or hedonistic and ethical man on one hand, and the religious man on the other hand.

In Europe there has been taking place in recent decades a humanistic renaissance, particularly in the Catholic Church.[2] This movement has led to a new discourse not only between Catholics and Protestants in terms of an inner ecumenism, but also between theistic and non-theistic humanists in terms of an external ecumenism. This discourse is a future oriented remembrance of past suffering with the practical intent of diminishing it. It does not proceed on the basis that its participants should give up their respective theistic or non-theistic thought concepts. It rather implies that the participants recognise the psychoanalytical insight that below what man consciously thinks there lies another dimension—that of what he feels. This inner feeling cannot be adequately expressed in words. But those who share the experience know that what they have in common is, indeed, more than what divides them, namely their different theoretical positions. What really matters for theistic and non-theistic humanists is not the difference between believers and non-believers, but between those who care for what torments people and those who do not. They have in common their feelings that there should be in all seriousness no war any longer, no hunger, no oppression, no destruction of external and internal nature, no alienation. Catholics who share this experience have become very open for the truth content not only of the Marxian social analysis, but also for the Freudian psychoanalysis in Europe as elsewhere.[3]

In present-day Europe the relationship between religion and psychoanalysis reflects itself most adequately in the non-theistic, humanistic critical theory of subject, society and history, in the Frankfurt School. The critical theorists combine psychoanalysis and historical materialism.[4] They stand on the Left of the Freudian movement, represented originally by W. Reich's early writings. They oppose passionately the Right of the psychoanalytical movement, represented by the Jungian, the cultural and the interpersonal schools. They are most popular today also among religious people in European advanced capitalistic society. Beyond this, critical theory is committed to negative theology in the tradition of Maimonides, Master Eckhart, and Nicolaus of Cusa. It is based on the Second Commandment: the prohibition to make images of the Absolute. It contains a mystical-revolutionary atheism for God's sake, an atheism in the Absolute. It is longing for perfect justice and absolute truth, which is not possible without the Absolute which guarantees it. It is the hope that the murderer will never triumph over the innocent victim. This negative theology is most beautifully expressed in the inscription on Horkheimer's gravestone, chosen by himself: 'In You, Eternal One, Alone I Trust!' (Ps. 91). The critical theory is essentially Jewish. The reconciliation between Christianity and Freudian psychoanalysis can happen only through the mediation of Judaism, which is the very source of both of them. Critical theory can help this mediation.

Today in Europe psychoanalysis is the most impressive philosophical ally of the Christian principle of subjective freedom in the struggle against a more and more positivistically administered society. Horkheimer and Adorno were always very much aware of the fact that their way of speaking about Freud as a philosopher would appear highly unorthodox to people for whom clinical psychoanalysis or Christian philosophy were everything.[5] Already the very notion of a Freudian philosophy seems to be almost a contradiction in terms. For the orthodox Freudian psychoanalysis is a positive science, which like all sciences today differentiates itself sharply from philosophy, not to speak of theology. The very word philosophy or theology connotes to the orthodox Freudian the rationalisation of unconscious wishes, the hypostatisation of wishful dreams and ideologies or something worse—paranoia. All these are the very object of Freudian analytical enlightenment. Without respect for existing taboos of European civil society Freud dares to look into the biological basement of the psyche and its libidinous and aggressive impulses and behind the façades of sublime philosophical and particularly theological ideals. He makes it his special task to reduce social and religious usages and attitudes to the biological drives of sexuality and aggression. The conflicts of these drives with the dominant familial, economic, political, international, and cultural structures of European bourgeois societies serve Freud as principles of explanation in the disenchantment of philosophical and theological 'essences', to which men like to trace back their motivations. Freud knows that the Jews are badly circumcised and that the Christians are badly christened. Freud was an inexorable enemy of intellectual superstructures as well as of metaphysical and theological hiding places and recesses of consciousness. Freud's credo was that there is no other source of knowledge about the world than the analytic working through of carefully tested observations. But Freud's negative attitude toward philosophical and theological illusions and delusions, so Horkheimer and Adorno argue rightly, is itself an expression of that particular mode of approach to the decisive problems of life (e.g., Eros and Thanatos) which critical theorists identify as philosophy or theology. Of course, in doing so the critical theorists must use the concept of philosophy and theology unconventionally, i.e., without the connotation of an idealisation of the horror and terror of the world as nature and particularly, as history. Contrary to such problematic ideological efforts there existed always in Europe another type of philosophy and theology. This critical philosophy and negative theology is characterised by the unconquerable conviction that without absolute truth there can be no truly human life. It is characterised by the will to make this truth without compromise into the guiding principle of one's life and to subordinate to this goal all personal interests. Furthermore, philosophy and theology means to the critical theorists the ability to make really new experiences, the energy to break through the hypnotic magic of ideologies, mythologies and idolatries, dominant in European late bourgeois and early socialist societies. Philosophy and theology means the ability to resist the deadening effects of the trivial daily routine on our capacity to perceive and to open up new horizons to our understanding of nature and humankind. Both motives, the passion for theoretical and practical truth and the ability to lead the human spirit to new heights rather of comprehension than of domination, belong to the definition of critical philosophy and negative theology. If the work of the thinker Freud is to be understood adequately then it is essential to emphasise its critical philosophical and negative theological aspect, which transcends all narrowly prescribed division of labour in the dimension of the positive sciences as well as all painful cleavages in Christianity and between Christianity and the other world religions. Freud, the critical philosopher and negative theologian, can more than the positive scientist help to build the bridge between psychoanalysis and good religion, one characterised by longing for perfect justice and absolute truth.[6]

Following Freud, Marcuse discovers in the development of Christianity a basic ambivalence between an image of domination and an image of emancipation.[7] Therefore he feels urged to re-evaluate Freud's theory in *The Future of an Illusion*, that the religious core idea of Divine Providence is an infantile illusion. The critical and extremely realistic philosopher and theologian Hegel thought of Providence as a very revolutionary notion.[8] Contrary to this, Freud stresses the role of this idea in the historical deflection of energy from the real improvement of the human condition to an imaginary world of eternal redemption. He thinks that the disappearance of this illusionary idea greatly accelerates the material and intellectual progress of humankind. Freud sees positive science as the great liberator from traditional, often evil, ideological religion. According to the critical theorist the function of science and religion as well as their interrelationship have changed in the decades since Freud's death. Within the total mobilisation of man and nature in European organised capitalistic society science has become one of the most destructive instruments of modern civilisation, destructive precisely of that reason and freedom which once it promised in its attack on positive religion. As the original promise of scientific enlightenment to free men from their fears and to make them into masters of their fate turned into a more and more abstract utopia, 'scientific' became almost identical with denouncing the earthly as well as the heavenly fulfillment. This precisely is the core of the present positivism (which does not even call itself this any longer, but rather critical rationalism) as the metaphysics of what is the case in European late bourgeois society. The scientistic attitude has long ceased to be the militant antagonist of positive religion (which on its part has equally effectively discarded its own explosive, prophetic, apocalyptic-eschatological remembrance and often merely accustoms people to a good conscience in the face of massive human suffering and death, guilt and meaninglessness). Adorno observes that bourgeois religion goes, strangely enough, but also not so strangely, very well along with the positivism dominant in Europe. Benjamin could characterise messianic theology with an abyss-like smile as being a small and ugly little hunchback and in any case unable to let itself be seen any longer in public. According to Marcuse, in the household of modern European culture the functions of science and religion have become complementary. Through their present usage they both deny equally the great longing and hope for perfect justice and absolute truth which they once aroused in masses of Europeans. They teach men instead to appreciate the facticity of a world of alienation and to adapt and conform to it no matter how great their cold feeling of meaninglessness, boredom and despair; there is simply nothing better to be had than this unjust, alienated reality. In this sense traditional positive religion is no longer the illusion for the critical theorist, which it once was for Marx and Freud. The academic promotion of traditional religion in European schools and universities falls very much in line with the predominantly positivistic trend and supports it and is supported by it and serves together with it the stability of the *status quo*. But Marcuse admits that where religion still preserves the uncompromising aspirations of freedom, peace, and happiness, as it happens today outside of Europe in the liberation theology of Nicaragua, El Salvador, Guatemala, etc., and inside of Europe in the critical political theology, religion's so-called 'illusions' have still a higher truth value than positivistic science, which still works for the elimination of religion.[9] Certainly the repressed utopian, apocalyptic-eschatological revolutionary content of religion, its exodus motifs, cannot be liberated by surrendering to the positivistic scientific attitude, expressed in some liberal theologies. But good religion—the identification with the innocent victim against the murderer—and critical psychoanalysis, as instrument of emancipation rather than adaptation, can very well co-operate toward a more rational and freer European society: a society in which the present apocalyptic contradictions between the religious and the secular, individual and collective, man and nature, man and woman, producer and consumer, owner and worker, rich and poor classes and countries, misery and luxury will be overcome.

According to Adorno, the theoretical construction of the separation between psychoanalysis and sociology which follows the dominant reality principle in European advanced capitalistic society must be corrected, since it neglects the critical zone where what is separated—individual and collective—come nevertheless seriously in touch with each other.[10] Not only the abstract, mechanical unity of the capitalistic reality principle binds together person and society and their scientific forms of reflection—psychoanalysis and sociology—but both of them never exist really in absolute separation. Thus for the critical theorist the most important, the most dangerous and therefore the most repressed moments of social reality—certain sexual or aggressive impulses—enter psychoanalysis, i.e., into subjective consciousness, after having been transformed into collective images. Freud related, e.g., the Zeppelin, as phallic symbol, to the dimension of archaic images. Only later C. G. Jung appropriated this Freudian discovery of archetypes into his individuation psychology, in order to take them completely out of the psychoanalytical dynamic and make them normative and thus transform them ultimately into clouding pseudo-mythologies.[11] Such Jungian imagery is the present form of myth in European society, heavily shared by conservative religious people. Europe has gone through the whole cycle from myth through enlightenment back to myth.[12] This form of Jungian myth encodes the social reality of European organised capitalistic society. Benjamin's conceptions of the dialectical images intended to penetrate theoretically this modern form of European myth.[13] For Adorno, as for Benjamin before, there is no doubt that the Jungian myths are indeed myths in the strict sense of the word. For this the critical theorists do not have to refer to the sympathy for European fascism, which Jung shared with M. Heidegger before and during World War II. The Jungian myths are indeed myths, since the transformation of the European social reality into the interiority of the individual and collective unconscious and thereby into something timeless, makes it untrue. The mythical imagery, verbally understood and accepted by European society, is necessary appearance and false consciousness, i.e., ideology. The shocks of modern critical art as well as of critical religion and theology which are directed against such imagery, intend now at last to explode that mythical untruth.[14] On the other hand, Adorno must admit that the myths of modernity are the truth in so far as the European late capitalistic society is itself a *mythos*, i.e., the old system of illusions and delusions. This truth element of the Jungian mythical imagery can be read out of dreams of modern Europeans. Even in their most distorted dreams these people know sometimes more truth, namely negative things, ideology-free content, about their neighbours, than under the control and censorship of their condition of being awake. The neighbours are in reality as they are in the dreams. Such is the modern European world!

The psychoanalyst Fromm predicts that today the only hope for people in European civilisation lies in the energising attraction of a new vision.[15] To propose this or that reform, which does not really change the system of European culture, society and personality, is useless in the long run since it does not carry with it the impelling force of a strong motivation. The concrete utopian goal, the reconciled society, is certainly more realistic than the realism of the present-day European conservative or social-democratic leadership. But the realisation of the new, more rational and freer society and man is possible only if the old capitalistic motivations of profit, power, domination, and instrumental understanding are replaced by new ones: being, sharing, tenderness, gratitude. The bourgeois marketing character must be replaced by a post-bourgeois creative and loving character. The cybernetic bourgeois religion must be replaced by a post-bourgeois messianic religion or by a radical humanistic spirit or by both. The critical theorist demands—like the critical political theologian—nothing less than an anthropological revolution as the basis for a social and cultural revolution in European late capitalistic society.

Fromm, like Horkheimer and Adorno, does not intend his demand for a non-theistic religiosity—obedience to the Second Commandment, negative theology, trust in the *Theon agnoton*—to be an attack on the positive religions existing in Europe today. But Fromm agrees with H. Küng and J. B. Metz, that the Catholic Church, beginning with its curia and bureaucracy, particularly the Congregation of the Doctrine of the Faith, the former Holy Inquisition, must convert itself to the spirit of Jesus as portrayed in the gospels.[16] Fromm thinks like Horkheimer of Jesus as the great Jewish prophet who died for all humans; who could not keep himself avariciously for himself; who belonged to all that suffers in nature and to all who suffer in society and history.[17] But Fromm overlooks like Horkheimer and Marcuse that Jesus is also the man who remained obedient to the God who showed himself powerless and abandoned him in deepest distress.

In Fromm's perspective nevertheless, European medieval culture flourished so well because people followed the Augustinian vision of the City of God. Modern European society bloomed for four centuries, because people were energised by the vision of the growth of the earthly City of Progress. Freudian psychoanalysis and Marxian social analysis belong to the last great fruits of this City of Progress. In the late twentieth century, however, this vision of the City of Progress is deteriorating to that of the Tower of Babel. It is now beginning, so the psychoanalyst Fromm predicts, to collapse and, if no help comes, will ultimately bury not only the Europeans, but everybody in its ruins. If the City of God and the earthly City of Progress were in terms of Hegel's dialectical logic of world history thesis and antithesis, a new synthesis is the only alternative to barbarism and chaos in Europe as elsewhere: the synthesis between the spiritual core of the European medieval world and the development of rational thought and science in the European modern world since the Renaissance. The psychoanalyst calls this new synthesis the City of Being. In this City of Being religious faith and psychoanalysis, redemption and happiness—as different as they may be—can be present nevertheless in each other and support each other and reproduce each other. Undamaged life can be lived.

Notes

1. A. Schmidt *Zur Idee der kritischen Theorie* (Frankfurt a.M. 1979) I-IV, pp. 36-126; A. Schmidt *Drei Studien über Materialismus* (Frankfurt a.M. 1979) pp. 81-134; *Der Stachel Freud* ed. B. Görlich *et al.* (Frankfurt a.M. 1980) part II; *Geselschaftliche Arbeit und Rationalisierung* ed. G. Brandt/Chr. Deutschmann (Opladen 1981) pp. 6-8, 8-56; R. J. Siebert *Horkheimer's Critical Sociology of Religion: The Relative and the Transcendent* (Washington D.C. 1979) chaps. III, IV, V, VI, VII, VIII; R. J. Siebert *From Critical Theory of Society to Theology of Communicative Praxis* (Washington D.C. 1979) chaps. I, II, III, IV, V, VI, VII, VIII; E. Fromm *Psychoanalysis and Religion* (New Haven 1971) vi-viii; chaps. III, IV, V; E. Fromm *Jenseits der Illusionen* (Hamburg 1981) chaps. 1, 2, 10, 11, 12; E. Fromm *Man for Himself* (Greenwich, Conn. 1966) v-viii; chaps. I, II, IV, V; W. Schmidt *Die Religion der Religionskritik* (Munchen 1972) chaps. I, III.

2. H. Küng *Infallible? An Inquiry* (Garden City, New York 1971) pp. 11-30; Th. W. Adorno, E. Kogon 'Offenbarung oder Autonome Vernunft' *Frankfurter Hefte* 13/5 (July 1958) 498.

3. H. Küng *Existiert Gott?* (München 1978) C, II, III.

4. Schmidt *Drei Studien*, cited in note 1, pp. 81-134; E. Fromm *Arbeiter und Angestellte am Vorabend des Dritten Reiches* (Stuttgart 1980) pp. 7-46, chap. I; Schmidt *Zur Idee*, cited in note 1, pp. 7-35, 125-142; E. Fromm *Jenseits der Illusionen* (Hamburg 1981) chaps. 2, 10; H. Marcuse *Kultur und Gesellschaft* (Frankfurt a.M. 1979) chap. III; Schmidt *Die Religion*, cited in note 1, chaps. 1, 2; *Der Stachel* ed. Görlich *et al.* cited in note 1, pp. 139-148, 149-178; M. Horkheimer *Die Sehnsucht nach dem ganz Anderen* (Hamburg 1970) pp. 40-47, 56-62, 67-70; S. Freud *Moses and Monotheism* (New York 1939) pp. 144-147; M. Horkheimer/Theodor W. Adorno *Dialektik der Aufklärung* (Frankfurt a.M. 1969) pp. 29-30; E. Fromm *To Have or to Be* (New York 1976) chap. III; Nicolas von Cusa *Wichtigste Schriften* (Frankfurt a.M. 1966) pp. 27-29, 31-33; Meister Eckhart *Traktate* (Stuttgart 1968) pp. 400-437; G. W. F. Hegel *Vorlesungen über die Geschichte der Philosophie* (Stuttgart-Bad Cannstatt 1965) pp. 131-132; K. Bloch *Denken heisst Überschreiten* (Frankfurt a.M. 1978) p. 317; J. Moltmann 'Theology of Mystical Experience' *Scottish Journal of Theology* vol. 32, 12; G. W. F. Hegel *System der Philosophie* (Stuttgart-Bad Cannstatt 1965) pp. 148-234; A. Schopenhauer *The World as Will and Representation* (New York 1966) chap. XXXII.

5. *Der Stachel* ed. Görlich *et al.*, cited in note 1, pp. 139-148.

6. Horkheimer *Notizen 1950-1969 und Dämmerung* (Frankfurt a.M. 1974) pp. 92-93; S. Freud *Moses and Monotheism* (New York 1939) pp. 142-160.

7. H. Marcuse *Eros and Civilization* (New York 1962) pp. 65-66; *Der Stachel* ed. Görlich *et al.*, cited in note 1, pp. 149-178, 186-192; S. Freud *The Future of an Illusion* (Garden City, New York 1964) pp. 26, 27, 41, 47, 52, 53, 69.

8. G. W. F. Hegel *Die Vernunft in der Geschichte* (Hamburg 1963) p. 46; G. W. F. Hegel *Vorlesungen über die Philosophie der Geschichte* (Frankfurt a.M. 1970) p. 369; G. W. F. Hegel *Frühe Schriften* (Frankfurt a.M. 1971) pp. 203-208; G. W. F. Hegel *Vorlesungen über die*

Geschichte der Philosophie (Frankfurt a.M. 1971) pp. 404-498; H. Küng *Menschwerdung Gottes* (Freiburg 1970) pp. 68-70; Th. W. Adorno/E. Kogon 'Offenbarung oder autonome Vernunft' *Frankfurter Hefte* 13/6 (June 1958) p. 397; W. Benjamin *Schriften I* (Frankfurt a.M. 1950) p. 494; W. Benjamin *Reflections* (New York 1978) pp. 312-313; W. Benjamin *Illuminations* (New York 1976) pp. 253-264, esp. 253; K. Marx *Early Writings* (New York 1964) pp. 43-44; S. Freud *Civilization and its Discontent* (New York 1962) pp. 11-20, 21-32.

9. J. C. Raines and Th. Dean *Marxism and Radical Religion* (Philadelphia 1970) pp. 9-10.

10. *Der Stachel* ed. Görlich *et al.*, cited in note 1, pp. 179-185.

11. *Ibid.* pp. 149-178; E. Fromm *Psychoanalysis and Religion* (New Haven 1971) chap. II.

12. M. Horkheimer/Th. W. Adorno *Dialektik der Aufklärung* (Frankfurt a.M. 1969) pp. 29-30.

13. W. Benjamin *Briefe* (Frankfurt a.M. 1978) II, pp. 671-683.

14. Raines *Marxism* cited in note 9, pp. 3-10; H. Marcuse *The Aesthetic Dimension* (Boston 1978) ix-xiii, chaps. I-V, pp. 71-73; *Der Stachel* ed. Görlich *et al.*, cited in note 1, pp. 119-139, 186-192; J. Habermas *Legitimation Crisis* (Boston 1975) pp. 117-130; M. Horkheimer *Eclipse of Reason* (New York 1974) chap. IV; E. Fromm 'Über Methode und Aufgabe einer analytischen Sozial-psychologie' *Zeitschrift für Sozialforschung* ed. M. Horkheimer (München 1970) pp. 28-54; Fromm *Arbeiter*, cited in note 4, pp. 51-79; J. B. Metz *Glaube in Geschichte und Gesellschaft* (Mainz 1978) pp. 29-43; J. B. Metz *Jenseits bürgerlicher Religion* (Mainz 1980) chaps. I, III.

15. E. Fromm *To Have or to Be* (New York 1976) chap. IX; Metz *Jenseits bürgerlicher Religion* cited in note 14, chap. III.

16. R. J. Siebert 'The Church of the Future—The Church From Below: Küng and Metz' *Cross Currents* 31, No. 1 (Spring 1981) pp. 62-84.

17. E. Fromm *The Dogma of Christ* (New York 1963) chaps. I, II, III; Horkheimer *Notizen*, cited in note 6, pp. 96-97; G. W. F. Hegel *Vorlesungen über die Philosophie der Religion*, cited in note 8, pp. 286-308; G. W. F. Hegel *Wissenschaft der Logik* (Hamburg 1963) I pp. 6, 20-21, 35-37, 87, 90; Hegel *Vorlesungen über die Philosophie der Geschichte* pp. 43-47, 568-569.

PART II

Particular Issues for the Dialogue

Steven Kepnes

Telling and Retelling: The Use of Narrative in Psychoanalysis and Religion

A rabbi, whose grandfather had been a disciple of the Baal Shem, was asked to tell a story. 'A story', he said, 'must be told in such way that it constitutes help in itself.' And he told: 'My grandfather was lame. Once they asked him to tell a story about his teacher. And he related how the holy Baal Shem used to hop and dance while he prayed. My grandfather rose as he spoke, and he was so swept away by his story that he himself began to hop and dance to show how the master had done. From that hour on he was cured of his lameness. That's the way to tell a story!'[1]

IN THIS narrative reported by Martin Buber in his *Tales of the Hasidim* the rabbi speaks of the curative powers of telling stories. The first patient of psychoanalysis, Anna O., also spoke of the curative powers of storytelling. She labelled psychoanalysis the 'talking cure' because she was helped by telling the tales of the traumatic events which led to her illness. Freud tells us: 'I begin the treatment, indeed, by asking the patient to give me the whole story of his life and illness.'

Psychoanalysis and religion are suspicious of each other on many issues; yet the two seem to find common ground when the issue of narrative is discussed. Recently, scholars of both psychoanalysis and religion are coming to similar conclusions in regard to narrative. They recognise that constructing and reconstructing, telling and retelling stories is at the heart of their respective enterprises.

Following the ground-breaking work of French linguistic psychoanalyst Jacques Lacan,[2] many psychoanalysts are rereading Freud with an eye toward his statements about language, interpretation, and narrative. Psychoanalysis is not portrayed as a medical science, based on the laws of mechanics or biology. It is presented as a hermeneutical discipline that interprets human signs and actions—a hermeneutical discipline for which the models of history and fiction are more appropriate than those of pure science. The 'new' psychoanalysis recognises that at the base of most personal signs and actions are certain themes and motifs; themes and motifs which are grounded in a personal story of 'root narrative'. Psychotherapy is the art of bringing this root narrative first to articulation and then retelling or interpreting it in such a way that new possible ways of being in the world are opened.

In both Jewish and Christian theology studies in narrative have blossomed as of late. Excitement about narrative is a logical extension of contemporary interest in myth, symbol, and metaphor.

'And the rabbi told. . . .' Telling is a most common activity for a rabbi. The Jewish tradition, founded as it is on certain primal or root narratives—the Genesis myth, the Exodus story, the Books of Job, Ruth, etc., has always valued stories and storytelling. Rabbis taught and teach by retelling or interpreting these root narratives. Talmudic literature is commonly divided into *aggada* and *halakah*, 'narrative' and 'law'. Yet even *halakah* is set down and interpreted through illustrative stories. As Lou Silberman suggests, Jewish theology has always been a 'narrative theology'.

In Christian studies the methods and techniques of the literary critic are replacing those of the historian in Biblical exegesis. The category of narrative has been important for new developments in systematic theology, political and liberation theologies, and Christian ethics.[3] Many have pointed out that Jesus was a 'rabbi' with a particular skill for telling tales. He perfected the art of the parable. The parables and the narratives of the life, death, and resurrection of Jesus, himself, are root narratives of the Christian tradition.

I would like to suggest that the first task of leaders of the Jewish and Christian communities, like their psychoanalytic contemporaries, is to articulate root narratives, here, root narratives of the religious traditions. In addition to this, and again like the psychoanalyst, religious leaders retell or interpret root narratives in such a way that new ways of being in a current situation are revealed.

I will review the use of narrative in psychoanalysis and religion, concentrating more on psychoanalysis in keeping with the emphasis of this project. I then will sketch some of the implications of the study of narrative for theology.

1. PSYCHOANALYSIS AND NARRATIVE

We are our stories. We are endless repetitions of our stories and we are endlessly repeating our stories. As the contemporary American psychoanalyst Roy Schafer points out, 'we are forever telling stories about ourselves'.[4] It is in these tellings that we constitute our selves. In addition, other selves are constituted for us through tellings. 'We narrate others just as we narrate selves. The other person, like the self, is not something one has or encounters as such, but is an existence one tells.'[5]

When we make a new acquaintance we ask the first questions of narrative: who, where, what, why? Why are you? Where do you live? What do you do? Why do you do it? We are forever inquiring after and relating narratives. All human beings have stories to tell and there even seems to be something like a desire to tell, an urge to communicate personal story. Most people communicate this story verbally, some do so through the plastic arts; but neurotics have trouble with direct verbal communication and they often communicate their story through the language of the body. Thus neurotic symptoms, somatic conversion reactions, obsessive rituals, and acting-out behaviours are manifested.

The neurotic is caught in a pathological repetition of a traumatic event, caught in the endless repetition of an infantile conflict. The neurotic is caught in the web of a theme, a part of a whole story.

The first task of psychoanalysis is to help neurotics to bring their acted-out stories to the level of verbal articulation. This articulation has a cathartic, curative effect. Joseph Breuer developed this story-telling cure with Anna O. and called it the 'cathartic method'. Freud supplemented Breuer's 'talking cure' with the method of 'free association'. He used both of these methods to explore the earliest life stories of his patients. Beyond this, he helped his patients to place these early episodes, these neurotically repeated partial themes, in the context of a whole life plot—what Freud called a 'case history'.

The entire process of psychoanalysis may be seen as a process of opening blockages of memory, correcting distortions, setting life events in proper sequence, and creating a coherent life narrative. This life narrative gives the patient a sense of past, present, and future, a sense of personal history and continuity, and thus a sense of self identity.

A crucial element in the process of establishing this life narrative is psychoanalytic interpretation. Interpretation introduces the elements of *change* and reconstruction into the patient's personal tale. An interpreted story is an altered story. And it is in the altering of personal tales that patients find possibilities for altering their understandings of themselves, their images of themselves, their identities, and their behaviours. For Roy Schafer, psychoanalytic interpretation occurs when the analyst retells the patient's tale 'along psychoanalytic lines'. Thus psychoanalytic interpretation is a retold tale.

The personal self, the personal story, of more traditional psychoanalysis possesses a 'static', 'monumental' quality. Freud likened the psychoanalyst to the archaeologist. Orthodox psychoanalysis appears as an attempt to excavate a buried self, a forgotten story. Once the barriers to memory are overcome and life story or 'case history' is formed, the self appears set. Many contemporary psychoanalysts are suggesting more fluid notions of life story.

The American psychologist Bertram Cohler proposes that all people maintain their sense of self order and meaning by successively reinterpreting and revising their life stories.[6] A life story, indeed an identity, is not a changeless monument; it is a series of stories, a series which includes stories which might be quite different at different times in our lives. Neurosis, in Cohler's scheme, is the result of the failure to renegotiate a new life story at times of personal crisis: the passage into adulthood or old age, a divorce, a job change.

Given the successive narrative revisions which are required to maintain order in times of change, our presentations of the past are often at odds with the 'actual occurrences'. Cohler complements the classic psychoanalytic position of historical determinism—past history determines present events—by suggesting that present events call for a revision of past history.

In constructing our lives as narratives we enter what I would like to call a 'narrative circle'. We use narratives to order our lives and we find that narratives begin to order and control us. Great or traumatic events require a reordering of our personal story and this story, in its turn, helps us to reorganise our lives and see new possibilities. This story proscribes and prescribes certain forms of action and behaviour.

Psychoanalytic discussion of the relation of self to story and story to behaviour is never complete if it fails to mention Jungian literature. To the extent that Freud is reinterpreted linguistically he is brought closer to Jungian psychology. James Hillman, the current leading Jungian interpreter, views the process of therapy as a process of 'revisioning story'. Hillman suggests that patients come to therapy with a variety of 'story maladies'. Some come because the leitmotif of their personal stories has broken down. Others come because they have no sense of 'plot' at all. Still others are condemned by 'abnormal stories' with bad endings. They have been 'written into a particular clinical fantasy', a clinical diagnosis of neurosis, schizophrenia, paranoia. They believe their lives cannot move from the parameters and patterns—the plots—these diagnoses represent. Hillman sees his patients as 'victims of their stories'. He suggests that successful therapy is a 'collaboration of fiction, a revisioning of story into a more intelligent, more imaginative plot'.[7]

2. RELIGION AND NARRATIVE: THE STORIES OF MARTIN BUBER

From the myriad of Jewish and Christian storytellers and story theorists I would like to focus on the narrative work of Martin Buber. Buber has been most frequently presented as a philosopher of religion or a religious existentialist and his narratives and thoughts on narrative have been little studied. A fresh look at Buber can be gained by examining his work from the perspective of narrative and hermeneutics. In addition, Buber uses narrative in novel ways and thus has a genuine contribution to make to contemporary discussions of the power and functions of story.[8]

What is particularly interesting about Buber's use of narrative in the light of the subject of this paper is that Buber highlights the 'event-character' of narrative. Buber, like Freud, views narrative as a way to retrieve significant life events. Where Freud focuses more on the ability of narrative to retrieve and overcome the desultory effects of traumatic events, Buber focuses on the ability of narrative to retrieve and celebrate the power of primal religious events—events in which individuals glance at the transcendent through the I-Thou relationship.

Buber presents his view of narrative in the prefaces to his Hasidic tales. Hasidism was a revivalistic and pietistic movement that flourished in the *shtetls* of East European Jews in the eighteenth century and Buber is largely responsible for bringing the literary expression of this movement to modern audiences. In his work Buber argues that Hasidic story has the capacity to embody holy events and communicate them to the present.

> Story is more than a reflection. The holy essence, it testifies to lives on it. The miracle that is told acquires new force; power that was once active is propagated in the living word and continues to be active—even after generations.[9]

Buber suggests that Hasidic legends about great events, by being retold, 'in themselves, became events'. As an event narrative is not merely a literary device, an illustration, or an example; it is an evocation, a recreation of an originative religious experience.

If relating religious events is a primary function of narrative it is not the only function which Buber describes. Narrative also has a didactic function. Buber remarks that the goal of a master Hasidic storyteller is to 'mix an event with a saying'. 'The event must be narrated with extreme caution in order that a saying may arise from it in pure spontaneity.'[10]

When we begin to speak of the use of narrative to relate a maxim, to relate wisdom, we begin to move into the realm of interpretation. When events are retold so that a maxim arises out of the telling, events are sometimes altered to better relate the maxim. In retelling, some of the facts are excluded or altered.

If we look at Buber's method for re-presenting Hasidic tales it is interesting to note that he did not merely present Hasidic stories in direct translation from Hebrew and Yiddish to German. Buber himself explains that he chose his tales from thousands of old pamphlets. He states that he edited the stories, even recast and reconstructed the stories: 'I received them and told them anew.'[11] Buber's tales must be considered retellings and interpretations of Hasidic tales. Here Buber is like the psychoanalyst who interprets by retelling his patient's tales. Thus, interpretation is shown to be a kind of retelling, a re-production of a new narrative.

But why did Buber choose to retell only certain Hasidic tales, and why did he alter and interpret these tales? In his 'Replies to My Critics',[12] Buber explains that he chose to focus on tales that reveal the interaction of the Hasidim and God in the mundane sphere. He chose to emphasise the Hasidic 'hallowing of the everyday', because he saw in this an answer to the spiritual problem of modernity. This is the problem of the disappearance of God from the secular sphere and everyday life.

What we witness here is the act of retelling, of interpreting traditional tales in the light of and for the sake of a contemporary religious situation. This parallels the process Cohler described wherein individuals retell or reinterpret their personal tales in the light of contemporary crises and events in their lives.

Just as individuals retell the story of their lives to cope with the vicissitudes of their contemporary situation, members of religious traditions retell the stories of their tradition to cope with the vicissitudes of the contemporary situation in which they live. Accordingly, we can expect that the narrative circle which I described in reviewing Cohler's theory of personal narrative and life course also obtains in religion. In both cases contemporary events order and reorder narrative and narrative orders and reorders contemporary life.

Buber's work illustrates that the contemporary situation often affects the way traditional stories are retold. On the other hand it is certainly true that stories of our religious traditions affect, order and reorder our religious lives. Indeed, most religious people live in accordance with the root narratives of their tradition. They derive a sense of order and meaning in their lives from these narratives.

Paul Tillich speaks of this process of deriving inspiration from tradition for our contemporary situation as the method of correlating religious message with current situation. More precisely, David Tracy indicates the importance of the whole process which I have described as the narrative circle by suggesting that theology employ a 'revised correlation method'. In Tracy's correlation method message not only answers and orders the contemporary situation but the situation often calls for a reordering of message.

The ultimate aim of the mutual orderings and reorderings of life and narrative that a revised correlation method or a narrative circle requires is the generation of new possible forms of personal and religious identity and new forms of being in the contemporary situation.

3. IMPLICATIONS FOR THEOLOGY

My review of the respective uses of narrative in psychoanalysis and religion has ostensibly covered methodological ground. Yet narrative is more than method. As I have indicated, narrative is not only a tool for psychoanalysis and an illustrative device for theology; it is crucial to the formation of personal and religious identity. In the same way that individuals form and are formed by narratives, religions form and are formed by narratives. Narrative re-presents the heart of religion, its originative religious events. Narrative re-presents a religious tradition—the valuable and essential elements of the past. The Baal Shem Tov says: 'Forgetfulness leads to exile. Remembrance is the secret of redemption.' It is through narrative that we remember the secrets of our traditions.

What a review of the nature of narrative suggests for theology is that telling and retelling stories is a crucial activity for the theologians. All of theology cannot be expressed by the narrating arts. Analytic categories, ethical and legal concepts are as important to theology as metapsychology is to psychoanalysis. Yet theory quickly becomes cold, brittle, and disembodied if it is not grounded in stories of suffering and joy, the events of selves and communities. Law—*halakah*—becomes abstract if it is not related to the concrete through story—through *aggada*. What Hasidic tales show is that an ethical law, a maxim can be related to concrete events in a narrative.

Yet narratives are not always productive. I have mentioned a narrative circle which puts event and story in creative tension. But it must be emphasised that it is easy to get caught in a vicious narrative circle—a circle in which pathological story and traumatic events feed each other in such a way that a horrible plot is constantly repeated. These re-enacted plots stifle human growth and creativity.

Neurosis can be seen as a pathological repetition of a traumatic story. Religious ritual is at times heartlessly repeated with no edifying result. Religious narratives are retold with no reference to the contemporary situation. Beyond this, with most startling results, entire cultures can be viewed repeating terrible plots—plots often supported by pathological repetitions of distorted psychological and religious narratives. Thus we witness the irrepressible and endlessly repeated 'plots' of anti-semitism, sexism, and racism. We witness the repetition of these traumatic and stifling stories and are dismayed by the horror of history relentlessly repeating itself. Freud had an apt phrase for what I have called the vicious narrative circle. He spoke of it as the 'compulsion to repeat', the 'death instinct'.

I would suggest that the activities of the theologian and the psychoanalyst merge in their similar attempts to combat vicious narrative circles, to combat the death instinct within individual psychology, within religion itself, and within culture. The first tactic in the combat is to encourage sufferers caught in the re-enactment of a horrible narrative to tell the story. Thus psychoanalysts encourage the tales of the traumatic events in the lives of neurotics. Thus theologians encourage the publication of the tales of oppressed minorities and women. Thus theologians encourage the tales of the survivors of Auschwitz. This first tactic is a movement in and for memory. The next tactic moves through the imagination. Here psychologists and theologians attempt an 'interpretive repetition', a retelling, what Hillman calls a 'revisioning of story'. Psychoanalysts and theologians attempt a revisioning of old pathological stories to suggest new possible forms of human interaction. They propose new visions for the future. In Paul Ricoeur's terms they propose 'paradigms for a new vision of reality'.

These new visions are most effective when they echo well-known and oft-repeated and interpreted themes of our traditional religious narratives. Here is the place for retelling religious narratives in accordance with the contemporary situation. Here we are able to connect to the past at the same time that we adapt to the present and open to the future. Here the full range of our temporal existence is comprehended. Here memory and imagination are connected and here we attempt to connect with God. In addressing those caught in the grip of a vicious narrative circle of death, we inspire change and give hope by telling and repeating the tales of sufferers and by retelling the tales of redemptive events in which God reached out in self-revelation to humanity.

Notes

1. Martin Buber *Tales of the Hasidim: Early Masters* trans. Olga Marx (New York 1947) pp. v-vi. The Baal Shem is the founder of Hasidism.

2. American interpreters differ from Lacan in their humanism, in their assertion of the existence of a 'substantial self'.

3. For an excellent quick review of the different positions on narrative in theology see David Tracy *The Analogical Imagination* (New York 1981) pp. 296-298.

4. Roy Schafer 'Narrative in the Psychoanalytic Dialogue' *Critical Inquiry* 7 (Autumn 1980) 29.

5. *Ibid.* p. 35.

6. Bertram Cohler 'Personal Narrative and the Life Course' Public lecture, University of Chicago, 9 November 1979.

7. James Hillman 'The Fiction of Case History: A Round' *Religion as Story* ed. James Wiggins (New York 1975) p. 140.

8. See my University of Chicago dissertation 'Martin Buber's Stories and Contemporary Narrative Theory'. Buber's novelty is to be found in a peculiar structural innovation in many of his stories wherein the 'middle' of the plot is made most important.

9. Buber in the work cited in note 1.

10. Martin Buber *For the Sake of Heaven* trans. L. Lewisohn (New York 1945) p. viii.

11. Martin Buber *The Legends of the Baal-Shem* trans. M. Freidman (New York 1969) p. 10.

12. Martin Buber 'Replies to My Critics' *The Philosophy of Martin Buber* eds. F. Schilpp and M. Freidman (La Salle 1967).

Carl Schneider

The End of Shame

> 'A Blush . . . is a very important spiritual experience.'
>
> Christopher Ricks
>
> 'A reticence, concealment, and restraint are among the prime conditions of religious and human culture.'
>
> G. Stanley Hall and Arthur Allin

1

AN EXCHANGE between philosopher Herbert Marcuse and theologian/critic Sam Keen succinctly encapsules the contemporary practical and theoretical issues relating to shame. Citing Marcuse's analysis of capitalism as a system that creates shamed and guilt-ridden personalities by psychological and political repression, Keen (1971) concludes that shame is an obstacle to the transformation of contemporary society: 'If shame and guilt cut off from our sensitivities, doesn't it follow that a revolutionary form of therapy would have to de-shame the individual?' Marcuse refuses to follow.

Marcuse: I think you have brought up the decisive point. I would say that shame is something positive and authentic. There are qualities and dimensions of the human being that are his own possessions—and I mean that in a non-exploitative and non-acquisitive way. They are his own and he shares them only with those whom he chooses. They do not belong to the community and they are not a public affair.

Keen: But you seem to be implying that only shame would protect privacy. Surely it is possible for an individual—a human being—to have privacy without shame.

Marcuse: I don't see how. . . .

In his pragmatic approach Keen captures the threat as well as the challenge of psychology to faith: in the name of personal liberation or societal transformation, we will develop a therapeutic technology to achieve the end (elimination) of shame altogether. In his neologism 'de-shame' we catch overtones of a de-programming technique which makes us shudder (itself a shame-related response).

Shame, repressive and inhibiting, is to be extirpated. This theme recurs not only in psychology, but in the major movements and issues of our day: pornography, feminism, political and personal liberation. Listen, for example, to two feminists, Kate Millett and Elinor Langer (1975), engage in a passionate exchange over the place of shame. Langer, reviewing Millett's book *Flying*, finds it an indecently confessional work. In reply, Millett argues that the book moves into a new humanity; *Flying* is an expression of that altered ethos. The new age has begun. 'Now we live and create it. Now we can speak it . . . dance it . . . bare it. . . . Unless we go back. Unless we grow ashamed.'

The new freedom is self-expression: 'it is shame that kept us silent.' Shame, she says contemptuously, is the 'absolute confirmation of "older notions and values and moralities"'. The conclusion: shame must be overthrown. The task is conceived in dramatic and violent metaphors because the need is not for revision, but for radical transformation:

> . . . a life one is not ashamed of, a life *against* shame, against even the very idea of it, the crime of it. . . . Heresy. Revolution. 'The shame is over,' concludes Millett.

Not often do we see the position expressed in such pure form. But similar, if less militant, sentiments are offered throughout contemporary psychology, especially in humanistic forms of psychotherapy. Fritz Perls (1969), the founder of Gestalt therapy and, before his death, resident therapist of Esalen Institute, calls shame and embarrassment the 'Quislings of the organism'. Dr Alexander Lowen (1979), the founder of yet another form of psychotherapy, bio-energetics, claims that shame 'rob(s) an individual of his dignity, of his self-respect'.

The positions in this debate are clear. The protagonists, however, are often unexpected. While Lowen, the founder of bio-energetics, laments the effect of shame, Stanley Keleman (1971), another well-known bio-energetic therapist and West Coast guru, comments: 'I see a positive side to shame and shyness—it's not all negative.'

Sometimes, indeed, the same individual is found on both sides of the fence. In a later essay in *Psychology Today* (1978), attacking Philip Zimbardo's book, *Shyness* (1977), and its advocacy of 'shyness clinics', Keen seems to have changed his tune about therapeutic technologies whose aim is to 'de-shame' people. Shame now appears to have a proper end. Shyness, that cousin of shame, he argues, 'is a special grace to be celebrated, rather than a disease to be cured . . . shyness guards the sanctuary of our privacy. . . . To value shyness is to cherish the interior life it protects. . . .' Perhaps Marcuse got through.

The reversals and divisions cited here reflect the confusion of current ideologies, and the lack of adequate grounding for much of our present day therapeutic technology. Much, however, of the contemporary estimate of shame is negative; shame and the realm of the private along with all oppressive forms and structures are perceived primarily as impediments to be overcome.

I have deliberately cited several examples from cult figures, mass circulation magazines, and popular culture to make the point that this issue is indeed a live one in contemporary culture. The same discussion, in more academic form, is repeated within the formal disciplines of psychology and theology.

Humanistic forms of psychology, because of their individualistic and expressive bias, are particularly prone to hold a negative estimate of shame. But psychoanalysis has also regarded shame as a fundamentally negative experience. Gerhard Piers, in his psychoanalytic classic, *Shame and Guilt* (1953), viewing shame as a product of tension between the ego and the ego-ideal, sees it as a response to failure and the shortcomings of the self in relation to the ego-ideal. This psychoanalytic formulation—shame as failure—in turn has been widely accepted in social psychology and anthropology. It is incorporated into Lynd's well-known work on shame, whose theme is that shame occurs along a strong-weak continuum, and has to do with a sense of smallness or inadequacy, a sense of not being good enough or acceptable. In shame, we perceive the self as *lacking*.

So viewed, the underlying dynamic of disgrace-shame is the fear of rejection. In psychoanalytic terminology, for the ego-ideal, this sense of inadequacy represents the threat of disapproval and ostracism.

Such explanations, however, have two shortcomings: they fail to direct attention to the positive component that accompanies being ashamed and they do not fit the '*sense of shame*'. There have been numerous studies of shame in modern psychology, but the characteristic feature of the great majority of them is their failure to acknowledge the positive dimension of shame, and attend to the sense of shame. This has been true no matter whether the studies have issued from humanistic psychology, psychoanalysis, or social psychology. It is a distortion which has directly affected the contemporary estimate of shame.

In almost all languages I have investigated, there are at least two words for shame. One for being ashamed, and the other for the sense of shame. The latter is akin to a sense of modesty or reticence. Julio Caro Baroja, for example, cites an aphorism regarding shame in Spanish society:

> 'Shame', as the Sages said, 'is the sign of timidity, which is born of true love.'

This shame cannot be adequately explained as fear of rejection. Rather, it is viewed as desirable because it is seen as exercising an appropriate restraint for the sake of a valued relationship.

The sense of shame, I have argued elsewhere (Schneider, 1977), is intrinsic to both our humanity and religiousness. True, there is also a digrace-shame which results from the exposure of some discrediting fact or quality. This being-ashamed is disruptive, disorienting, and elicits a painful self-consciousness. Yet it is a mistake to view even this shame as simply negative in the sense that we would be more fully human were it eliminated. Rather, shame has a fundamentally relational, revelatory character. In the blush of shame, the undivided self in action gives way to the doubled self. Shame is an act of self-attention. As Silvan Tomkins (1963) has recognised, 'In contrast to all other affects, shame is an experience of the self by the self'. This intimate link between shame and self-discovery led Helen Merrell Lynd to title her essay 'On Shame and the Search for Identity'. Through the experience of shame, identity may not only be confirmed, but shaped, enlarged, and put into perspective.

Silvan Tomkins notes that shame is 'two-valued and therefore deeply disturbing'. In contempt, the object—self or other—is simply rejected; in shame we still seek a relationship. In shame the object from which we are alienated is one with which we still sustain a positive cathexis.

Even disgrace-shame is 'deeply ambivalent': it is an 'act of facial communication reduction in which excitement or enjoyment is only incompletely reduced'. This conflict is most easily seen in young children who cover their face before a stranger, but who also peek through their fingers. Tomkins is almost alone in recognising this ambivalence. This ambivalence is of the essence of shame. While shame may separate the self from the other, it also points to a deeper connection.

The recognition, or lack of recognition, of this positive dimension deeply affects one's interpretation and evaluation of shame. On the one hand, there are those psychologists and social philosophers, from Plato to Paul Goodman, who see shame as intrinsic to human existence, treat its manifestations with delicacy and respect, and perceive its humanising and pedagogical function. In contrast, those who regard shame as artificial, repressive, and essentially a social-control mechanism and who are most impressed with its pathological and destructive manifestations, focus on the negative judgment in shame and overlook the deeper positive dimension. Many theorists who so regard shame have conceptualised it primarily in terms of such factors as failure, inadequacy, incompetence, loss of control, and stigma. Such formulations fail to identify the central aspect of shame.

Shame, at its core, is intimately linked to *the human need to cover that which is exposed*. This is delightfully reflected in the Indo-European linguistic roots from which our words for shame derive. The Lithuanian word for shame, for example, belongs to a cluster of words which includes our English words *custody*, *hide*, *house*, *hut*, *shoe* and *sky*, all of which have descended from an Indo-European root *(s)que-; *(s)qewa-, which means 'to cover'. A second Indo-European root *(s)kem-; *(s)kam-, also meaning 'to cover', gives us both our English word *shame* as well as the English *camera*, the French *chemise*, and the German *Hemd*.

Behind the biblical expression, 'the shame of their nakedness', lies the assumption that the exposure of that which should be covered is shameful. It is, of course, not only sexual matters that call for a proper privacy. Some covering of nakedness needs to be present in all human encounter since, as Bachelard put it so well, to be human is to be 'a half-open being', partly exposed and partly covered. All experience is potentially vulnerable to violation and thus potentially in need of protection. An element of reticence is thus always present and appropriate to human relationships, including one's relation to oneself. To ignore or to deny this is to be shameless. Nietzsche gave eloquent expression to this: 'We no longer believe that truth remains truth when the veils are withdrawn. . . . Today we consider it a matter of decency not to wish to see everything naked . . . or to understand and "know" everything. . . . One should have more respect for the bashfulness with which nature has hidden. . . .'

Bonhoeffer is the theologian who speaks profoundly of shame as the symbol of our separation. In most human meeting language provides the cover. When human speech unfolds as it should, language is more than talk, explanation, or chatter. It expresses and yet stops short of an unspoken depth and fullness of experience. Language both discloses and covers in all encounter. Respect for this depth and resonance of human meeting is the sense of shame.

This dialectic of covering and uncovering, moreover, is at the heart of religion. *Religion may be understood as the dialectic of covering and uncovering of the sacred in time and space*. When either dimension is lost, religion is deformed. In our own period, religion, along with other aspects of our culture, has been under the sway of an ideology of discovery and exposure.

Oblivious to the need for the tacit, reticence, and covering, contemporary society has collapsed the dialectic, and knows how to value only disclosure, demythologising, unmasking. The erosion of the sense of shame has produced a preoccupation with uncovering and the explicit. This bias needs to be redressed. Mystery is as central to religion as is revelation.

The acknowledgement of the value of a proper sense of shame would be part of such a rebalancing. Shame is a symbolic covering of that which is exposed. The modern desire to tear away all the veils is an act akin to robbery or rape. A sense of shame respects the veiled nature of truth. The shared conventions of a culture that embody its collective sense of shame are indispensable protections and do much to define the quality of human life in a society.

An adequate hermeneutic of shame would recognise the dialectic of covering and uncovering that is intrinsic to human existence and to our experience of the sacred. This dialectic appears not only in such discrete phenomena as the Ark of the Covenant or Yahweh's passing by Moses, but even more in the very power of human utterance. Speech refers beyond itself. Speech is the symbolisation of human experience. At the same time that it gives explicit expression to that experience, it also reminds us of how much of reality's fullness remains unvoiced and implicit. In articulating some themes, it remains mute to others.

An adequate hermeneutic of shame would recognise the hidden-shown character of consciousness, language, and the sacred. It would not fall sway to a truncated ideology of individualism and the explicit. The treatment of shame, then, would involve the two-fold task of recognising the positive role of shame in covering as indispensable in human experience while criticising false shame and prudishness as impediments to true community. This two-fold task would be akin to Ricoeur's concept of a double hermeneutic, of both interpretation as the manifestation and recollection of meaning, and interpretation as demystification, the exercise of suspicion. It would involve a dynamic interplay between covering and uncovering, between the hidden and shown, between a respectful sense of shame before what Ricoeur (1967) calls the 'opaque transparency' of the religious symbol, and a shameless deciphering of religion as a mask.

My argument, I believe, is analogous to that made by Robert Kegan in his essay 'There the Dance is: Religious Dimensions of a Developmental Framework' (1980). What I refer to as the dialectic of covering and uncovering Kegan speaks of in terms of the universal tension between limit and possibility, between differentiation and integration, between autonomy and participation. Kegan argues eloquently that to grasp only one side of these universal tensions is to embrace only part of the truth and to find oneself operating out of a skewed anthropology.

This is, I believe, what is finally at issue in the struggle to define the nature of shame and its proper end: the anthropology we hold. Those who understand shame as an impediment to the realisation of our humanity and wish to see its end (*finis*) are, I believe, caught in the sway of a truncated ideology of individualism and the explicit. We saw this in the Keen-Marcuse and the Millet-Langer exchanges. Sartre and Nietzsche, I believe, more fully embody this bias in their treatment of shame. Their doctrine of the solitary and self-sufficient self leads them to reject shame. Nietzsche's perception of the shamelessness of God and Sartre's humiliation before the Other are ultimately symptoms of their inadequate anthropology. For them, that one is knowable is a threat to one's existence.

Our age rejects shame because it rejects our bond with the Other. We believe, falsely, in the liberation of the autonomous self. The recovery of a proper sense of shame would go hand in hand with our acknowledgment of our inherent sociality. The sense of shame reminds us of the deep mutual involvement we have with one another. The recovery and acknowledgment of such inter-relatedness would lead us back from our pursuit of the path of an autonomous individualism. Our discomfort with shame reflects our lack of comfort with the reality of our interdependence. The determination to cast off shame in our culture is grounded in a distorted individualism and rationalism. The point is not to throw out shame and enthrone autonomy and reason, but to recover an appropriate sense of shame and of the mutuality that is its foundation.

Shame symbolises our mutual involvement. It also reminds us of the dividedness and estrangement that characterise that involvement. To refuse to acknowledge this broken character of our lives leaves us open to that which is demonic and destructive. Because we know ourselves incapable of living together in a community of complete trust and openness more than momentarily, shame is and will be always in order as the mark of our vulnerability as selves both separate from and belonging to a larger Whole.

Bibliography

Keen, Sam 'Deliver us from Shyness Clinics' *Psychology Today* (March 1978) 18f.

Keen, Sam 'An Interview with Herbert Marcuse' *Psychology Today* (February 1971) 37-38.

Kegan, Robert G. 'There the Dance Is: Religious Dimensions of a Developmental Framework' in *Toward Moral and Religious Maturity: The First International Conference on Moral and Religious Development* ed. James W. Fowler and Antoine Vergote (Morristown, N.J. 1980) pp. 403-440.

Keleman, Stanley *Sexuality, Self and Survival* (San Francisco 1971).

Lowen, Alexander *Pleasure: A Creative Approach to Life* (New York 1975).

Millet, Kate 'Forum: "The Shame is Over"' *Ms.* 3 (January 1975) 27-29.

Nietzsche, F. *The Gay Science* trans. by Walter Kaufmann (New York 1974).

Nietzsche, F. *Thus Spoke Zarathustra* trans. by Walter Kaufmann *The Portable Nietzsche* (New York 1954).

Perls, F. S. *Ego, Hunger and Aggression* (New York 1969).

Piers, Gerhard, and Singer, Milton B. *Shame and Guilt: A Psychoanalytic and a Cultural Study* (Springfield, Ill. 1953; reprinted ed. New York 1971).

Schneider, Carl D. *Shame, Exposure and Privacy* (Boston 1977).

Tomkins, Silvan *Affect Imagery Consciousness*, vol. 2: *The Negative Affects* (New York 1963).

Zimbardo, Philip G. 'Misunderstanding Shyness: The Counterattack' *Psychology Today* (June 1978) 17ff.

Zimbardo, Philip G. *Shyness: What It Is, What To Do About It* (Reading, Mass. 1977).

Donald Evans

Can Christian Teaching Be Good News about Sex?

IN A popular book entitled *The Good News about Sex*,[1] Father David Knight says that for Christians sexual intercourse can be sacramental, bringing not only a union between two persons but also a union between them and God. Since within each person is God's life and love, 'when they communicate themselves to one another they are communicating God'.[2] For Knight, sexual intercourse as sacramental can be a 'graced action' like a loving smile: 'If I smile, that smile is literally both human and divine. It is a graced smile. The person I smile at is being smiled at by God. . . . I am expressing through my smile an infinite, divine act of love. And it is *my* act of love. Because God has united me to himself as His own body, his act of love is my own. This is what a graced action is: it is one and the same action which is both God's personal act and a human personal act. . . . This is what sexual love is between Christians: one act of love, both human and divine, made flesh. The awesome thing about Christian sexual expression is that God is expressing himself in everything we do. But if this awe inhibits us, makes sex solemn, then we haven't understood how human God becomes in us. In the playfulness, the teasing, the sexiness of sex, God is expressing himself. The physical expression of love between Christian couples is hilarious and holy, sexy and sacred, playful and sacramental all at the same time. Whether sex is awesome and profound or teasing and light, every sexual encounter between Christian married couples is a mystery both human and divine.'[3]

Would that this were so. Very few Christians actually experience sexual intercourse as a sensuously delightful bodily pleasure, a mutual expression of love unmixed with other emotions, a union of two spirits merging together, and a sacrament in which every action, including orgasm, is both human and divine. On the contrary, many Christians still feel guilty about enjoying sexual pleasure. Almost all feel negative emotions during sex, or else repress them. Few have any awareness at all of their own spirit as an abundance of vital energy within and around them, and even fewer are aware of the sexual dimension of this energy or the merging of spirit with spirit during intercourse. Few have any idea of how to practise the continuous surrender of self to God which is required if every action is to be God's action, and of those who do, even fewer can include sexual intercourse in this sacramental way of life.

Why is there such a gap between contemporary Christian theory at its best and contemporary Christian practice? One explanation of the lack of *delight* in sex is the detrimental influence of much traditional Christian theory about sex as an essentially animal urge, justifiable only as a means of procreation within marriage, and otherwise to be dominated by reason and transcended in spirit—for Catholics ideally in a celibate life. In practice the main way by which most Christians have been induced to confine their sex to marriage has been through guilt concerning sexual desire as such, not only outside marriage but also within it. Many people today reject such Christian puritanism, but although such rejection is a necessary first step it is often a dead end, for the 'liberated' person often retains a puritan understanding of sex as nothing but the animal urge for pleasurable sensations of physical intimacy. The puritan suppresses such sex as alien and the 'liberated' opponent rightly accepts it as something human, but both limit sex to the body, and sex remains largely disassociated from emotion and remote from heartfelt love and spiritual union and surrender to God.

This constricted awareness of sex affects many Christians, whether they accept puritanism or reject it. A few have a vision of sex as a delightful bodily pleasure, a loving spiritual union and a sacramental participation in divine love, but they do not know how to move towards that goal. Unfortunately the practical guidance which they receive from the Church is usually superficial, for it assumes that conventional Christian practices will suffice. There is usually little indication that an arduous and lengthy process of profound personal transformation is necessary. At best Christians are taught that marriage is a school of character, but the main virtue to be learned is a heroic fidelity in which, as Rosemary Haughton says, 'people stick out a hard life together, not stopping too much to wonder if they are fulfilled'.[4] Now it is true that the main merit of marriage is that the mutual commitment provides a necessary context for working through the radical changes in character which must occur if each person is to be a relatively unimpeded channel of the divine love, not only to each other but also to others—including their children if they should decide to have children.[5] But fidelity as a dogged determination to stick together is at best only a necessary condition for the growth of more expansive, life-affirming virtues which enable two people to rejoice in each other as the sacramental presence of God. And if the call to heroic fidelity is heard as an end in itself, it typically degenerates into an obstacle to growth, a refusal to expect any growth towards the expansive virtues not only in one's partner but also in oneself. Marriage, whether Christian or non-Christian, is typically a mediocre compromise in which two people secretly and stoically contract not to disturb their delicate balance of limited mutual expectations by raising questions about the meagre love, especially the meagre sexual love, which exists between them. Alternatively, if stoic resignation fails and the marriage breaks up and each person looks elsewhere for a more loving relationship, the new relationship is rarely radically different from the old one, for the same basic complaint, conscious or unconscious, is carried over: 'You don't love me enough, so I can't love you.' Whether the complaint is stifled by stoicism or surfaces to provoke separation it is the basic obstacle to growth towards Knight's ideal. The pervasive sense that 'You won't or can't love me enough' which each person brings to *any* intimacy prevents each person both from accepting whatever limited love is actually being offered by the other and from giving love to the other. So two love-starved people either heroically resolve to stick together or part in bitterness and blame.

Some people are of course less dominated by this pervasive and perverse attitude than other people, and so their marriages or separations are less bleak. But there is a strong tendency towards this attitude in everyone, and it is not seriously challenged by conventional Christian practices. Three radical conversions in self-understanding must occur: psychological, spiritual and sacramental. Each conversion brings a new insight:

(*a*) *Psychological insight:* 'When I say, "*You* don't love me enough", I don't really mean you but rather my mother as I experienced her when I was an infant. I've been confusing her and you. When I forgive her I can forgive you. And in sex I can now be physically and emotionally intimate with you without confusing you with her. And when I forgive her I can forgive not only you but also God for my being born, and then I can receive the love which is actually being given to me.'

(*b*) *Spiritual insight:* 'I have been dependent on you to feel alive, but now I realise that I am already full of abundant life, vital spiritual energy, which radiates from me, especially towards you. And I realise that I want to merge spiritually with you, especially in sexual intimacy. None of this depends on how much you love me at the moment. My love for you is an overflow of an excess of life-energy which I am delighted to share.'

(*c*) *Sacramental insight:* 'Regardless of whether any human being loves me I participate in God's love as a channel through which it flows to others. I now realise that love is not mine to possess or give. Love is God living me in every action, including sexual intercourse.'

Each insight comes only as the outcome of a lengthy and strenuous ascetic discipline. The psychological discipline involves re-living some very painful repressed childhood experiences and uncovering dark, destructive impulses within oneself. The spiritual discipline involves breaking down 'armouring' in the body and the emotions so as to awaken consciousness of spiritual energy and allow it to flow unobstructed, for example between the genitals and the heart and the top of the head. The sacramental discipline involves the death of Narcissus, the self-centred self which resists being lived by God, so that in surrender to God one may live from moment to moment the paradox of grace, 'I, yet not I . . .'. The death of Narcissus is necessary if the psychological and spiritual disciplines are to play their properly subordinate roles, enabling us to experience the full scope of the self which is being lived by God, and clearing away the formidable inner obstacles to surrender of that whole self. Without sacramental discipline the other disciplines degenerate into an endless, self-preoccupied quest for an illusory 'fulfillment' in separation from God. Indeed, the most fundamental criticism of contemporary western psychology from a genuinely Christian perspective—or more broadly from a genuinely religious perspective—is that it reinforces Narcissus.[6]

Christian tradition has rich resources on which to draw in teaching sacramental discipline, *except* in its application to sexual intercourse. This colossal exception is no accident. The practice of continuous self-surrender to God in every action has been developed and taught mainly among contemplatives who are celibate. So the human actions which have been experienced sacramentally as divine actions have not typically included what Knight calls 'the playfulness, the teasing, the sexiness of sex'. There is in fact a dearth of practical Christian teaching concerning how to realise what Knight describes. Personally I have found more enlightenment concerning this from a non-Christian contemplative, Da Free John,[7] who is not a celibate and who does not split off spirit from body and sex. His profound wisdom concerning these and other matters could greatly enrich Christian thought and practice. In this essay, however, I have been asked to focus on *psychological* challenges to Christian faith concerning sex, so I will turn to the psychological discipline to outline its discoveries.

When people re-experience their own infancy and also observe infants without censoring what they see, it becomes evident that sexual desires begin then. In infancy there is an intense longing for bodily and emotional intimacy, and both belong together. Typically the longing for intimacy is in conflict with an accompanying terror lest intimacy mean being overwhelmed in total dependency. And since the longing for intimacy is not satisfied there is not only an affectionate tenderness, expressed in mutual caresses, but also rage and grief and fear of rejection. Why is the longing not satisfied? There are two main reasons. First, the parents bring to the infant their own impediments to loving intimacy, impediments which began for them in early infancy. These vary greatly from person to person, but no parents are perfect, and all have some impediments, especially some narcissism. Second, even if the parents were ideal, the infant has a tendency to narcissism ('The world must revolve around me to satisfy me') which makes its desires insatiable, limitless and impossible to fulfill.

Infants differ considerably in the 'strategy' which they adopt to deal with disappointment in sexual love. In my book *Struggle and Fulfillment*[8] I distinguish five common strategies: anxiety or chronic agitation and inner pressure, hostile and resentful wariness, idolatrous addiction to substitute satisfactions, masochistic despair which gets pleasure out of pain, and stoic detachment which self-deceitfully says, 'I didn't want it anyway'. The turbulent passions and distrustful strategies to which sexual desire gives rise in infancy do not disappear, but are buried in the unconscious where they continue to operate secretly as the child becomes an adult. They are stirred towards the surface of consciousness when once again—this time in sexual intercourse—flesh touches flesh all over. In addition to infantile longing and infantile tenderness there are also conflicting feelings directed towards the sexual partner: terror and rage and grief and fear of rejection. There are also narcissistic demands that the sexual partner exist entirely for oneself, and bitter resentment because he or she does not. And he or she is also dealt with in accordance with one of the strategies which began in infancy—anxiety or wariness or addiction or masochism or dispassionate detachment. If detachment dominates one may succeed in repressing almost all the unconscious emotions which sex has carried with it in the body's nervous system since infancy. Thus one can treat sex solely as a physical pleasure disassociated from emotion. But this is a self-deception. Sex is intrinsically or naturally a longing for emotional and bodily intimacy, a longing which is present in every human being, and the sexual gestures of tender caressing and bodily intimacy are inherently linked with affection. Moreover, sex is also unavoidably associated with the passions and strategies which I have indicated. All these elements are infantile in origin and character. They can be largely replaced by mature love, but this transformation requires a psychological discipline which exposes the perpetual conflict between insatiable longings for intimacy and self-created barriers against intimacy. Contemporary psychotherapy at its best provides such a discipline, and nothing else does it as effectively. Although elements in it were discerned in many cultures prior to Freud, he and his successors have provided an essentially new approach in human self-understanding, especially concerning sex.[9] Loving sex is rare not because sex is merely an animal appetite which is inherently unloving, but because for humans sex is largely an ambivalent emotional attachment which began in infancy.

Psychological discipline can also reveal that we transfer passions and strategies from infancy not only to our sexual partners but also towards God. The passions and strategies are pervasive in scope, for they began when mother was the whole world and they continue towards the whole world, and especially towards whatever underlying reality unites that world—that is, towards what we unconsciously view as God. Whether or not we consciously believe in God, we have unconscious feelings and attitudes towards God. In *Struggle and Fulfillment* I showed how five distrustful infantile strategies are directed towards God and how these undermine five forms of trust or religious faith which also begin in infancy. In general, sexual distrust and religious distrust are very closely related, as are their opposites.

Thus some psychologies provide a basis for psychological discipline in ways which affect both sex and faith. Others do this for what I have called 'spiritual discipline', which is virtually absent from Christian tradition. The main psychologies providing disciplines by which one may become aware of spirit *as spiritual body* are western secular accounts originating from Wilhelm Reich[10] and eastern religious accounts drawing on tantric Hindu and/or Buddhist traditions.[11] Both Reich and tantra need to be revised, in different ways, for Christian use, but both can help Christians to bridge the current chasm between sexuality and spirituality.

Notes

1. David Knight *The Good News About Sex* (Cincinnati 1979).
2. *Ibid.* p. 99.
3. *Ibid.* pp. 94-95.
4. Rosemary Haughton 'Marriage: An Old, New Fairy Tale' in *A Curious Tradition: Marriage Among Christians* ed. James Burtchaell (Notre Dame 1977) p. 143, quoted in Stanley Hauerwas *A Community of Character* (Notre Dame 1981) p. 192.
5. For reasons partly indicated in this essay it seems obvious to me that Christian marriage can be a vocation and sacrament in the absence of the ability or the intention to have children. Indeed, the decision to have children should not be implied in marriage, but should be distinct, for not all couples who are ready to begin to grow through marriage are ready for parenting.
6. On this see Jacob Needleman *A Sense of the Cosmos* (New York 1975). In a recent book he also criticises exoteric Christianity for reinforcing narcissism: *Lost Christianity*.
7. Da Free John *Compulsory Dancing* and *Love of the Two-Armed Form* (Clearlake Highlands, California 1978).
8. Donald Evans *Struggle and Fulfillment* (London 1979 and Philidelphia 1981).
9. For an excellent non-technical and elementary introduction within the Freudian tradition see Allan Fromme *The Ability to Love* (New York 1966). For a superb psychoanalytic account of the infantile origins of male chauvinism see Dorothy Dinnerstein *The Mermaid and the Minotaur*.
10. See Wilhelm Reich *The Murder of Christ* (New York 1953) and his innovative follower, Alexander Lowen *Depression and the Body* (Baltimore 1973). For tantra see Bernard Gunther *Neo-Tantra: Bhagwan Shree Rajneesh on Sex, Love, Prayer and Transcendence* (New York 1980).
11. Da Free John is very illuminating concerning all this.

Jack Dominian

The Challenge of Psychology to the Practice of Faith

INTRODUCTION

IN THIS article I do not propose to treat in any detail the theories of Freud, Jung, Adler, Erikson, Klein, the neo-Freudians such as Horney, Fromm, Sullivan or the group of their eminent successors. I would like to draw attention to the fact that the derivatives of these theories have spread widely throughout the world, in various forms of psychotherapies and also in counselling, and the results of these forms of help have profound implications for the practice of faith.

The importance of psychoanalytic theories and individual techniques belong to technical manuals. Here I want to examine the experiences that everybody undergoes whatever form of psychotherapy is used. I want to begin by stressing the importance of the basic principles of all psychotherapy, namely the one-to-one relationship (or the particular intimacy of a group) with the specific characteristics of empathetic, non-advisory, non-judgmental listening and the implications for caring and loving.

1. THE BASIC PRINCIPLES OF ALL PSYCHOTHERAPY

(*a*) Empathetic Listening

The person who enters into analysis, psychotherapy (individual or group) or counselling receives the unique experience of being listened to with concentrated attention and in a manner which gradually reveals to him that his inner world is actually understood, not only in terms of intellectual concepts but also in the way he feels. For many people this is a startling experience which they may never have experienced before. At home, school, in the parish at confession they were not often listened to in any depth and, if they were, frequently only their reasoning was attended to. Their feelings and emotions were often not only ignored but actively discouraged. In psychotherapy they are being received, often for the first time, as a *whole* person and inevitably feel that this reception is more consistent with being loved than anything they have known before.

This listening has other qualities as well. It is regular and reliable and has a predictable quality. Unlike all other caring relations, psychotherapists are present week in, week out, except for holidays and illness. Their realiability parallels parental and spouse presence at its best and, since most patients have not had one or the other or both, the therapist provides them with the first opportunity of such continuous, reliable and predictable experience of unconditional acceptance, trust and availability. The nearest equivalent person in the structure of the Church is, of course, the priest. But he, in no way, can function in the way the therapist does and so there begins one of the earliest adverse comparisons between care in the Church and in psychotherapy.

This is, however, a superficial comparison. For behind the limitations of the available Church lies the ever present covenant between God and man and the Bible emphasises repeatedly God's continuous, reliable and predictable availability. What we can learn from psychotherapy is that this availability of the therapist is but a symbol of God's characteristics present in the Church as a whole and in the sacraments in particular.

This particular spiritual truth is difficult to grasp because God's availability has a quality of mystery, the mystery of the unseen and the unknown; whereas the therapist is visible and his presence immediately realisable. It is, however, the acquaintance in depth of a significant other, represented by the therapist, which gradually allows us to learn to feel personal presence in its physical absence. Many patients start therapy by finding it extremely difficult to retain the awareness of their therapist the moment they depart from his room. Gradually they learn to retain his features, words and the feelings awakened for longer periods until they can internalise his presence in his physical absence.

This sense of internalising a significant other is crucial to spiritual experience. Some men and women possess a very strong sense of the presence of God in their life, many do not. Those who undergo therapy learn to internalise their therapist who becomes their god. But this capacity to make present can and does extend beyond therapy and allows us to acquire the sense of internalising the Significant Other which is Jesus Christ in and through the scriptures, the sacraments and our neighbour.

A profound awareness of an-other who is a real person, deepens and refines our sense of perception of others in their physical absence and therefore helps us with the perennial problem of becoming aware of the invisible God. Too many people who undergo therapy can become so enchanted with the deep sense of personal caring they experience at the hands of the visible therapist that they lose all sense or interest in the divine and the symbolic equivalent of care. Indeed, part of the current disenchantment with the sense of God is the enormous influence that the gratification of the concrete and visible has over the mind of man.

(*b*) Non-Advisory and Non-Judgmental Listening

All those who undergo therapy reach their therapist with years of being received by parents, teachers, priests who passed judgment on their ideas and gave them instructions of what to do and how to become better persons. This sequence of events may have been linked with feelings of guilt, incompetence and helplessness. Their mentors were all well-meaning people who passed on the teaching of the Church, the wisdom of society and their individual experiences. These instructions were often absolute and left little room for individual evaluation or judgment.

In therapy this whole world changes. Advice and judgment are replaced by interpretation. At first the absence of direction can be frightening and, indeed, for some people intolerable. But gradually a new world enters into the fabric of life. The patient loses the sense of being a naughty child and the sense of goodness now emerges from their own internal awareness and evaluation. The sense of guilt, infantility and helplessness is replaced by reality, adulthood and self control. A marvellous feeling of taking charge of one's life gradually unfolds and the thrill of the sensation gives temporarily a gratifying experience of omnipotence. Men and women, who have laboured for years to find themselves in the midst of feeling bad, guilty, incompetent and helpless, gradually come to realise that they have found themselves and they are none of these stigmatised things. It is not surprising that some of them receive their liberation and crown the process of this achievement by repudiating authority, rules and the sense of badness, often giving up going to confession which is a painful reminder of all that they have come through.

This sense of emancipation from weakness, guilt, badness and constant tuition of how to be good is not only realised in therapy, although it finds a powerful exposition there. When experienced superficially it is linked with one of the false promises of our age which is that man can rise above dependence and take complete charge of his own life.

In fact an effective and successful therapy manages to take the patient out of the stage of infantile fear and leads to a world of adult responsibility. Adult responsibility does not mean that perfection has been reached. It does not mean that reality has replaced sin: but it does mean that guilt is no longer easily aroused over minor instinctual transgressions of aggressive and sexual feelings, failure of duty or from the fear of challenging authority. Rather a deeper sense of the failure to love one self, our neighbour and God results. Transgression becomes a matter of the failure to love the whole of ourself and that of our neighbour. The emphasis shifts from acts of commission to omission. There is a deeper sense of the dignity and meaning of being human and the failure to realise its potential. Ideally the Christian should reach a deeper sense of the invitation to be as perfect as our Heavenly Father and the psychological truth of St John's first epistle where he stresses the incompatability between fear and love (1 John 4:18).

2. THE IMPLICATIONS FOR CARING AND LOVING

(*a*) Sexuality

Reference has been made to sexual transgression. Many people who have undergone therapy have done so before the current age of sexual liberation and emancipation had taken hold of western society. Thus they were often burdened by a deep sense of guilt with regard to such matters as masturbation, sexual thoughts, phantasies and the contravening of the strict sexual ethics of Christianity and particularly of the Roman Catholic Church.

In the course of therapy they will have come to realise how much of this sexual world is natural to men and women. The forbidden, the suppressed, the guilt ridden emerges and gradually assumes a different meaning. Despite superficial criticisms, it is not true that a competent analyst will directly or indirectly hint that the separation between sex and guilt is a signal for uncontrolled sexual behaviour. Nowhere does Freudian or any other theory become a licence for immorality. But patients, trapped in the claims of inhibition and suppression, feel—in the early waking of sexual freedom—an urge to behave sexually in a manner they would never have dreamed of tolerating prior to therapy. This is more a consequence of *discovering* their sexuality than *abusing* it but, in the process, much traditional teaching may be temporarily overruled. Furthermore, such fundamental values as celibacy, chastity, rules against masturbation and the restriction upon acting out sexual variations—particularly homosexuality—may all be questioned. If fear of authority recedes, then the previously forbidden is now released both from instinctual restraint and intellectual submission. The combination of acting out the forbidden and questioning the case that authority has made against it can temporarily lead to all sorts of sexual extravaganza.

But any deep and successful therapy not only dissociates excessive guilt from the sexual dimension of behaviour, not only traces the roots of infantile sexuality but also enhances a deeper sense of the whole person. Ultimately the separated elements of the self are gradually brought together and no successful analysis leaves the patient with an effective process of reduction with little or no integration of the separate parts of the self. Jungian analysis is particularly strong in this but it is a goal for which most therapies aim. In this process of integration the sexual takes its place with the rest of the self. Instincts alone do not represent men and women. Instincts separated from care, trust, concern and love leave the person partial, incomplete and ultimately deeply dissatisfied. A successful therapy lifts sex out of the morass of guilty instinctual isolation and integrates it with the other energies of the personality which seek similar values of worth in inter-personal exchanges of love with others.

Thus the Christian deepens and enhances his sexuality as it is freed from its instinctual isolation and becomes integrated with love, love of self and of others. The passage to this point may be prolonged and stormy but ultimately it is a goal which is worth achieving.

(*b*) Aggression

Many of the same points can be said about aggression. Traditional Christianity has laid emphasis on the meek and mild Son of God. It has discouraged aggression which has often been seen as defiance of authority and so a good deal of aggression directed towards parents, teachers, the Church has been suppressed, a feature that many patients bring to therapy. In their phantasies these men and women have felt guilty about expressing their aggression which has been associated with fears of killing, destroying, damaging and injuring others, particularly members of the family.

As with sexuality, aggression is gradually freed from its guilty associations. Once again all hell may be let loose. The timid and tolerant become aggressive and hostile. The suppressed rage explodes and in this early phase of release the occasions, boundaries and limitations of expression have yet to be learned. Many critics of therapy—and indeed many patients themselves—are frightened by the release of such energy. Furthermore, if everybody expressed their anger spontaneously then, it is asked, how can the principles of peace and love, cherished in the Christian tradition, be protected?

Clearly the release of aggressive feelings from repression, suppression and guilt is not meant to facilitate uncontrolled and irresponsible aggression. It does mean, however, that men and women acquire the *freedom* to become angry when an important issue is at stake. We need to protect the essentials of our identity from assault by others. We need to show at times to our neighbour that he or she is hurting or damaging us in an unacceptable way. Anger is needed to protect an important value. Just as with sexuality, psychological theory is no licence for hatred and hostility. But it does give the freedom to be angry without guilt when this is essential. Even our Lord showed moderate and extreme anger, showing us that it has a place in human integrity.

But just as sexuality can temporarily go out of control, so can the expression of aggression. It takes time to acquire the freedom of expressing anger and then using it only on appropriate occasions. But when this is learned, so much hidden hostility—expressed in criticism, teasing, irony, sarcasm, resentment and acts of destruction—disappear because resentment, frustration and genuine hurt do not remain as festering wounds in the psyche. It is only when we are genuinely free to express anger that we can learn to control it fully and have a genuine chance to pursue the peace that Christ gives us.

(*c*) Family, Dependence and the Church

One of the links between early childhood experience and the Church is the common language of father for priest, mother for some nuns, brothers and sisters for religious orders and ultimately holy father for the pope. These terms were linked in many with the ideas of obedience and dependence. Parents are obeyed as figures of authority and so were priests and nuns. Both are linked with a system of authority and for all Catholics submission to the teaching of the Church is a principal feature of the practice of their faith with ultimate acceptance of the authority and teaching of the pope.

In the family structure, experiences of dependence are linked with trust and security and the same characteristics were present in the wider family of the Church. If the ordinary Roman Catholic was prepared to remain dependent on the teaching of the Church, then he or she lived in an atmosphere of calm and security with the confidence of a young child that mother Church would provide all that is spiritually necessary for salvation.

Thus, both in the life of the family and that of the Church, there operated social and psychological systems whereby a continuous dependence and submission was the price to be paid for security. This view of peace and security has been shattered by the social and psychological drive for autonomy. Throughout the world there has swept a hunger for social and political independence and, in the field of psychology, autonomy, self-control and independent evaluation have replaced the values of dependence, blind obedience and submission to authority.

In therapy the individual gradually emancipates himself/herself from the superego and internalised elements of parental and other authority. The ego gradually emerges as a self-evaluating, directing and independent person. The guilt of disobedience is replaced by the affirmation of self expression. The frustration of dependence gives way to the confirmation of autonomous self-esteem.

These psychological movements of emancipation find their way into the practice of faith. Wherever this was an expression of infantile spiritual dependence, psychological autonomy and severance of acknowledgment of parents may be linked with the giving up of the faith. Just as parents become redundant, so do their spiritual equivalents. Such faith is indeed the universal neurosis of the projected father on God that Freud postulated. If one is given up so is the other.

But the relationship between child and parent is one of gradual separation in which the emerging adult is always equal in worth as a person to the parent and the ultimate goal of family life is to facilitate the growth of mature, responsible and autonomous adults. The same applies to the Church. The Church is the people of God and its integrity depends on the integrity of each and every one of its members. Despite previous patterns, the Church needs mature Christians who relate to the hierarchy in an inter-personal encounter of equality of worth but difference in function. Neither blind obedience nor empty submission is desirable for the health of the Church or the encounter between man and God. God invites us to love him and love can only be realised in the presence of the fullest possible wholeness of the individual, a wholeness which psychotherapy has facilitated in a unique way.

CONCLUSION

In the depths of all forms of psychotherapy there is a seeking of discovering and integrating elements of the self which are unrecognised, destructive or incomplete. This is truly an attempt to bring about human wholeness which in turn reflects more accurately the image of God in man. Wholeness by itself is not enough because it is detached from the source of its origin which is God. It is only when wholeness, accomplished by psychological means, is linked with its source that holiness is achieved and this is the ultimate goal of all authentic human reorganisation achieved psychologically.

Sebastian Moore

Death as the Delimiting of Desire: A Key Concept for Soteriology

JESUS REPRESENTS the new human being, in whom desire is liberated from its capitivity in dread (mortality), anxiety (hunger), and shame (sexuality), and in the consequent split between self-love (thus split within itself) and self-gift. The cosmic loneliness, from which all the above complexities and weakenings follow, is replaced by an intimacy with the grounding mystery that all scholars—believers and non-believers—agree to have been unique: the awesome, enigmatic, often threatening mystery which our loneliness makes God into, becomes Abba. And from this intimacy there flows the liberation of desire as a boundless hope permeating all experience, within the self and with other selves. This is the mind of Jesus.

A very important question then arises. What would be the effect of this new experience of being alive on the men and women whom Jesus drew into a close discipleship? It would be to liberate in them the boundless desire. In them, too, the inner loneliness began to burn with desire and hope. And 'God' began to mean, uniquely, the object of this hope, the undoer of all loneliness: this, rather than the many things God appears as to the spirit caught in its loneliness—that never quite trusted blend of promise and threat that we all remember from a religious childhood. 'God' begins to take on God's *real* infinity, namely as the only satisfaction for *infinite desire*. In terms of religious tradition, this 'caught' religiousness of Jesus was a total revolution. One contemporary theologian speaks here of the 'contagion' of Jesus.

And now comes perhaps the biggest question of all. Granted that they were thus lifted into a new intensity of desire, a new concentration of boundless desire in hope, how did they stand in relation to the three factors *that make for* cosmic loneliness: hunger, sexuality, and mortality? Not being *radically* liberated, as Jesus was (that is, not being 'without sin'), they were still a prey to the immemorially human anxiety, shame and dread. There would be a strange, unprecedented tension between the new liberating simplicity that they were catching from the sinless one and the universal condition of humankind.

Thus the liberation caught from Jesus at this stage could only be a beginning. The basic anxieties of human existence still presented an agenda. Some distinct further engagement with them would have to take place if the liberation from cosmic loneliness was to be carried through.

To consider the negotiation of this further stage, I shall narrow the agenda to the item called mortality. By far the most important reason for this is as follows. We do not interact with our mortality as we do with our hunger and our sexuality. Unlike its two partners, death is not experienced by us. We do not know anyone who has died, still less have we *direct* experience of death. This means that our negotiation of our mortality is radically incomplete—*and this goes for Jesus too*. The reason, then, for concentrating the theological investigation on the mortality factor as we embark on the disciples' 'further stage' is the awesome one that here Jesus too is 'incomplete', not perfected. So radical is the challenge that mortality offers to our spiritual journey, that it remains outstanding for the Master as well as for the disciple during the 'first period' of the story, the first act of the drama.

But having made this decision, we have to review the whole meaning of death.

My starting-point here is a hint I took recently from a philosopher friend. Clearly, he said, the two most important things about us are, that we desire and that we die: isn't it curious, he continued, that no philosophy really tries to find a connection between them.

I want to suggest what the connection is, and why we do not readily see it. Desire is boundless. We are never satisfied. Everyone knows this. It is a truism. Now if we look at the myths in which humankind expresses its feeling about death—the Jewish Sheol and the pagan Hades for instance—we find that it is thought of as the falling-away of all connections, all ties, all bonds, a dissolving of that complex web whereby we are woven into this world. Now bonds, connections, ties, *are limits*. So this intuitive sense of death as the dissolving of ties implies the falling-away of limits. And this implies—though the implication is never followed-up—the liberation of desire. Now the reason why this implication is not followed-up is that we tend never to recognise head-on the limitlessness of desire. We *show* that we are never satisfied, by our movement on from one desire-object to another, but we prefer to create the temporary expectation that the new object *will* satisfy. And so the limitlessness of desire is not a direct experience but an implication—and a disturbing one—woven into all our living. (It is perhaps only in contemplative prayer, that Abbot Chapman brilliantly characterised as 'an idiotic state', that we have some experience of limitless, formless desire. Which of course is why this state is better for us than any other.)

The affinity of desire with death is hidden from us because in the thought *of both* we brush against infinity, and that scares us. We are deterred from holding in focus the affinity between desire and death.

And if *in our thinking* the two do not readily come together, how much more are they separated *in our living*. The point—already made—about our having no experience of dying, is that we have no experience of the *encounter* between our ongoing, desire-driven life, and death. We do not know the encounter between limitless desire and delimiting death. We do not know death *as* the delimiting of desire.

Now it is just such an experience—how produced if producible at all—that is needed to complete the process of liberation of desire as initiated by the ministry of Jesus. I said at the beginning that the disciples needed a 'further engagement' with the factors making for our cosmic loneliness. What I have just described is that 'further engagement' with the mortality factor, to which, it will be remembered, I have narrowed-down the inquiry. And let me recall, too, that this further engagement is required in Jesus also, for he too must perforce live short of death, short of the encounter between desire and death.

Let us see, then, whether such an experience was, in the circumstances, possible. First let us recall what it is that, in normal circumstances—in all but those unique circumstances—puts the experience beyond our reach. There are two causes of this: first, the fact that we do not experience death; second, the fact that we do not *directly* experience the limitlessness of desire. In other words, *neither* party to the desire-death encounter is present for us.

Now *one* of these factors *was* present for the disciples of Jesus. As we have seen, he awoke in them the sense of limitless desire. This was the heart of the 'Palestinian' experience: the lyric of God's universal love, of the kingdom on the way. The subjective component of the ministry of Jesus is the awakening of our limitless desire from the immemorial sleep of its cultural accommodation.

But so much beyond our normal capacity-to-handle was this liberated desire that it could not have 'worked' for them *except* as crystallised in Jesus as in a symbolic focus. We know this phenomenon, in a less intense form, in all movements stirred up by a leader with charisma. The followers are being so awakened, their horizon so expanded, that they cannot 'handle themselves' except with the leader as their focus for feeling. And some scripture scholars are very helpful here when they pinpoint the dynamic of Jesus' ministry thus: He seemed to be awakening something that is in all people but that only worked in consort with him. (Dunne's *Jesus and the Spirit*, one of the best recent works in this area, makes this very point.)

Now let us recall the second obstacle to the anticipation of death: the fact that not only infinite desire, but also death, is absent from the meeting—in normal circumstances. But if, in the privileged circumstances we are considering, infinite desire *is* present but is perforce symbolically constellated, concentrated, focused, *outside* themselves and *in* Jesus, then the destruction *of Jesus* will be, for them, the meeting (experienced as a collision, but a meeting nonetheless) of desire with death. Jesus, their desire, was brought to a horrible end—even common language accepts the description of Jesus as 'their desire'.

In their experience, then, of Jesus taken from them and put to death, they underwent *that* loosening of desire from its context that we call 'this world' which we *shall* undergo when we come to die. No other people have had this experience of dying while yet alive. And all who have had an experience of dying, while yet alive—and how really this happens in a bereavement—have had an experience of which the disciples' experience is the 'prime analogate'.

His death was their death. It put them on 'the other side'. It projected their desire beyond time and space to where alone desire can be satisfied. It brought desire and death into the same reference-frame. They knew what the dead know. Death was no longer the shadow that broods over the only life we know. It had been gone through. There is in this experience a radical spaciousness of the soul, a totally new capacity to perceive. The mystics have a taste of it, in the dark night of the soul.

But now comes the most important question of all. Is this new capacity the condition of total fulfillment, of the ultimate bliss, of the final freedom? On the contrary, it carries a *need* that is as broad as the soul itself now is. Death as such does not introduce into the blissful presence: it only readies the soul for it, and the readying is a total emptying, a desolation. No real theism is compatible with a concept of death as simple breakthrough. Finite and infinite do not unite in that way.

The awful end of Jesus, then, causes that total emptying of the soul which is the indispensable threshold for union with the infinite. We are in 'the middle way', the dark night of the soul. How then does the 'third moment' come? What is the manner of the succeeding union?

It has two components, subjective and objective. Subjective: God, who alone is abundant life on the other side of death, moves in them as an unspeakable joy and peace. They taste infinite Spirit—and in their description of the Resurrection encounter they speak much of the Holy Spirit, its indispensable presence to the encounter. Objective: They encounter Jesus, as the focus of their *new* life as he was the focus of their new desire in the old life. We recall that he too had to be brought to the crisis of death, to death as the 'critical mass' of desire. The interweaving of his need with theirs is, at this stage, very close. Where he needs to be brought to death for *his own* perfecting is precisely where he fails *them*, projects them into the dark night. Therefore *his* perfecting in the new life will be the focus of *their* rallying on the other side of death. And how often we pick up this rhythm in the kerygma: the crucified one, the failed one, the Godforsaken one, is raised up in glory. Its undertone is: that which let us down is what has lifted us up. This is the meaning of the glory of Jesus, of which the visual component is but a metaphor or perhaps psychic projection: his working after death (his) in the souls of men and women what only God works, his supporting, with a presence that can only be divine, the souls that have lost all power, all human resources, in the wilderness of death. He supports them with the divine Spirit life that is now his.

He shines on the dead, who alone have eyes for him. He harrows hell, which alone is deep enough for him. He fills our emptiness, which is infinite and knows him who alone can fill it. He is Alpha and Omega, was dead (bringing us to death) and lives (bringing us into life), and holds the keys of death and hell.

This is risenness from the dead. The sight of him *raises* the dead, raises the seer from the ranks of the dead into which he has been introduced by the awesome Passion. It was impossible for him to be seen without the seer being thus raised. And who are the dead? They are the to us unimaginable *subject* of the emptiness, the shadowy people of the emptiness, the people who are empty of all that fills us, the empty-handed. The pagan Hades, the Jewish Sheol, express this shadowiness of the dead when *compared* with us the living—obviously a distortion but a very human one. He who for us *fills* the emptiness, he who for us is *life* in the emptiness, who makes the emptiness vibrate with God, cannot be where we think of the dead as being.

The condition of the disciple, of being dead, is found in the pure state in the Good Friday interim. With the Easter experience, however, it remains as that which is filled, as the abiding and always re-entered prerequisite of the filling, as the foundational helplessness of the enSpirited being, as the helplessness into which we must ever sink back, in a crisis of spiritual challenge, to be lifted up with Christ in the Spirit. The emptiness of which I am speaking is precisely that powerlessness of which Paul continually speaks—'When I am weak, then I am strong'. It is the state of death, of disconnection, of losing all hold on things. The whole Pauline doctrine of weakness as the seat of the Power is located there. It appeals, ultimately, to that never-to-be-forgotten moment when Jesus was taken away from them for a fate that could not be in doubt. It appeals to that primordial collapse of our hold on life.

We are at the heart of what might be called the 'clean sweep thinking' of Paul. For Paul, *everything* is swept away, the past annihilated, 'sin destroyed in the flesh', the decree against us nailed to the cross and wiped out, and so *all* is new, God is all in all: the total emptiness admits the infinite in power; the experienced disconnection of death is transformed by the encounter with the one who wakes the dead. All Paul's soteriology, the sense that everything pours away on the gibbet of the new man, is in this great rhythm of emptying and filling, emptying of all, filling with 'glory'. For what is 'glory' but life in limitless abundance? How easily our stultified modern imagination sticks at the visual connotation of 'glory'!

The Pauline rhythm appears in the literary parallelism such as 'died for our sins, raised again for our justification'. This is far more than literary or rhetorical: its balance is not aesthetic. It is not a case of 'two sides of the same coin'. What is referred to is the massive *sequence* of emptying ('died for our sins', the taking-away movement) and filling ('rose again for our justification'). The statement that Christ 'died to sin' is a compact, a compendious statement, collapsing into one the death of Jesus and its immediate emptying effect. He 'dies us to sin, to the old world'.

The Pauline statement that 'the world is crucified to me and I to the world' is another way of referring to the total disconnection-with-all that the Jesus-crucifixion effects for the disciple. The mystical teacher *enjoins* 'detachment' from the world. Paul, in the power of the Spirit, *announces* 'crucifixion' of our relationship with it, doing to our relationship with the world what our death *will* do to it and what only Jesus' death, now, *can* do to it. Paul's doctrine of 'death to self' can now be better understood. Normally, we take 'self' to mean selfishness, and 'death' as negative, the destroying, the ending of selfishness. But 'death to self' refers to the original disciple-experience, in which death (the real death we *shall* die) comes to the *desiring* self as the latter's crisis of transformation. 'Death to self' means 'the delimiting of desire by death'.

His death brought them to 'the other side'. But it is not that, once you are on the other side, you necessarily 'see what's there'—Jesus in glory. The other side *as such* is empty, formless, helpless. There has to be the quickening of the dead soul by the living Jesus, by the 'life-giving Spirit' that, on one occasion, Jesus is said to have *become*. The preparation for this enlivening is not the effecting of it.

Gone is the old opposition between a 'theologia crucis' and a 'theologia gloriae'. Once the Golgotha experience of the disciple is seen as creating that total emptiness in which alone the glory can appear, the opposition loses all meaning.

How the new life can pass into the *convert* to Christ, the early pagans for instance, needs to be considered; though I have no difficulty in seeing how *contagious* must have been the new life which God was manifestly bringing out of their death for the *first* heralds. And it is obviously significant that the convert had to *die* into the new life, in Baptism. Would that our image of Baptism could recover its original vitality and shed that notion of tokenism that sacraments perhaps inevitably acquire in the impoverished climate of the now played-out Enlightenment, in which we still have to live.

Jesus says, in John, that the dead will hear the voice of the Son of God. Only the dead *can* hear that voice in its own accent. But only those who have *begun* to hear it, and then lost it, can *be* dead.

Ignatius speaks of 'consolation without a cause'. It is perhaps his most penetrating description of the mystical, of that deep sense in us whose stirring can only be from God. The Golgotha experience of the disciple sweeps away all 'causes'—and we may use that world also in the sense of 'things worth working for'—so that there can come upon the soul that reality which is wholly and absolutely its own. 'Consolation without a cause' is 'life where there has been only death'.

In conclusion, I might dare to add a ninth beatitude. Blessed are the dead, for they shall be raised up to renew the earth. There is the danger that my heavy concentration on the psychology of the disciples will lead to a confinement of the Resurrection to psychology, to the neglect of its dimension of earth-renewal. But those who through the unique Jesus sequence *knew death*, knew what only the dead know, touched our very constitution in existence, touched our cosmology. And knowing the glory of their Master in that foundation of the world, they knew that the world itself was transformed. Otto Ranke has said 'We are born beyond psychology and we die beyond psychology'. At the centre of world history, a small group of otherwise undistinguished people were led out on to that awesome promontory which is 'beyond psychology' and, through the life that there met and filled them, changed the world.

Coda

Crucial to this account has been the notion of death as a falling-away of all ties. This is classically described by Rilke in the latter part of his first Duina Elegy ('True, it is strange to inhabit the earth no longer').

Now this idea of death is by itself enormously depressing. It does not by itself connote a breaking-free. It only connotes freedom if desire is fired with a supernatural hope, which it only *can* be definitively by Jesus Christ filling the infinite emptiness of death with the Holy Spirit of the all-originating.

Still, infinitely depressing though it is without this presence of Jesus, the notion of death as the falling-away of all ties and meaning is the prerequisite to any possibility of faith in that presence. This notion of death is *not* one of extinction, but of a carrying to infinity of the loneliness in us. The notion of death as extinction is not only incompatible—obviously—with the Resurrection faith. More importantly, it is not that which the Resurrection faith displaces. Rather it expresses such a state of inattention to the self as cannot even raise the question of faith. I cannot think of myself as not existing. Certainly I can think of a world in which I do not exist. Of course a logician would object here 'You cannot think of *anything* as not existing. But the things about which you now think *will* cease to exist. So, then, will you'. I am not clear as to how to answer this, but I am pretty certain that the answer has to do with the great divide between those who think self-awareness is the same as self-reflection and that the self therefore has to be summoned to awareness as does Iceland or the Titanic, and those who know that this is not so. Somehow, the inalienable quality of self-awareness stretches, to our mind, 'beyond the grave'. And those whose more *reflective* mind is faithful to this inalienable quality envisage themselves, however depressingly or vaguely, 'beyond the grave'.

It has been suggested to me that my notion of death as a falling-away of all connections is the Jewish notion, in so far as there can be said to be one Jewish notion. It is of great help to me to hear this. There is something seriously wrong about the statement, frequently made by Christians, that the Jewish scriptures in the main have no idea of survival. Were this so, Jewish religiousness could not be that highly self-aware religiousness that we know it to be. And if it is true, as I have argued, that the Resurrection faith addresses itself not primarily to a fear of extinction but to the gloomy survival of Sheol or Hades, then I would expect *that* faith to which Christ offers a wonderful opening-out to *have* a concept of survival, and not a hopeful one. The Jewish idea of Sheol is a true idea of the state after death without Christ, without the Resurrection. We have lost this capacity to think of 'survival without fulfilment', because our Christian habit of mind packages together survival and fulfilment in face of a materialistic culture that denies both. And of course Pascal's 'wager' works on the supposition that they are one. If there is no God, well, you won't be the loser by your pious moral existence, for there won't be any more you. This distorts and privatises the Christian hope. The meaning of the traditional belief that Jesus saves us from hell is, that if there is no God and Jesus and Holy Spirit we are all going to hell—which C. D. Broad, commenting on spiritualistic phenomena, said resembled nothing so much as a modern university!

In short, there is a fatal confusion, in the Christian mind, between 'survival' and 'blissful survival'. It is the latter that our faith offers *in contradistinction to the former*. The hope of a blissful immortality arises not from death as foreseen and speculated about, or as 'revealed' about, but from death as anticipated by the disciple of the Crucified, who becomes alive to the taste of Christ in the Spirit of the eternal ground of being. The Gospel is addressed to an emptiness, that *underlies* this life and *is all of* the next: an emptiness that must be entered willingly, with desire, for the Spirit to fill it with eternal life.

PART III

The Debate on Therapeutic Consciousness

E. Doyle McCarthy

Psychologising Religious Faith: A Sociological Overview

SOCIOLOGISTS OF contemporary culture have identified the tendency of modern individuals to experience their social institutions as man-made constructions, structures reducible to human subjectivity and intentionality. It was the German social philosopher Arnold Gehlen who studied the social psychological implications of this development. Gehlen argued that given the changing character of modern institutions, individuals lack a stable and encompassing 'background' (*Hintergrundserfüllung*) for action—a consistent set of unquestioned meanings through which to relate themselves to their world. Modernity deinstitutionalises; it divests social life of its stabilising qualities and its grounding in the shared sentiments of a large collective body. As a result the matrices of meaning which traditionally gave purpose to human action—culture, religion, and work—have been weakened or diffused. These developments have been the subject of study for sociologists of modern culture who, like Gehlen, have associated the weakening of the religious sector (called the process of secularisation) with a second development: the emergence of emotional subjectivism and the translation of religion into personal belief and morality. Related to this is the tendency to view the individual subject as the source of authority and, in Daniel Bell's words, to root all justification 'in the demands of the "I", of the "imperial self"'.

Gehlen called the process of turning inward *subjectivisation*: the opening up of a wide 'foreground' in which human knowledge is marked by reflective reason. Expressions of subjectivisation abound in the so-called 'turn to the subject' in modern art, philosophy and literature, each of which expresses, within the intellectual and artistic sensibility, a new sophisticated awareness of psychic phenomena. But its basis is to be found in the structures of modern consciousness itself, a change in the realm of human psychology. From this standpoint, modern psychology and psychoanalysis are seen as developments responding to the changing structures of human consciousness, or as modes of understanding and describing in systematic fashion modern psychological reality. Psychoanalytic theory is, then, like a finely tuned lens which focuses on the newly elaborated structures and processes of the modern psyche and its heightened capacity for introspection.

From the standpoint of the sociology of knowledge (here, the sociology of modern knowledge) the psychologising tendencies of contemporary religious bodies can be seen as inherently secularising. In the works of the sociologists Peter Berger, Thomas

Luckmann, and Daniel Bell, psychological modes of interpreting religious belief, sentiment, and action are indicative of a substantive shift in the understanding of religion itself. In the case of contemporary religious belief, it is precisely because the social world of religion has lost its once dominant place that traditional religious meanings and values have had to be translated into a contemporary idiom—in this case, one which has held a central place within today's culture generally—psychology. Peter Berger argues that secularism as a world view means the denial of transcendence. Psychology translates transcendent phenomena into terms of immanence: 'self realisation' and 'mental health'. In a similar vein, Daniel Bell has written that the force of religion does not derive from either self-interest or individual need. Ironically, in its modern variant, psychologised religion forces the individual back within himself. The crisis of belief becomes part of the drama of self.

From the works of these authors certain themes concerning contemporary religious belief emerge. These include: first, the tendency within contemporary society for religion to be understood as a 'personal belief' and for morality to be defined as 'private'; second, the anti-authoritarian shaping of doctrine, theology, and religious practice within the churches; third, the contemporary emphasis on the values of 'feeling', self-gratification, and self-fulfilment and, coupled with this, the tendency of individuals to seek out direct, emotional experience for self-validation generally, and as a means for 'finding God', in particular; fourth, the translation of traditional moral language into a psychological and clinical one and the redefinition of questions of morality into those of mental health.

Secularising processes affect various social groups and classes differently (a subject of innumerable studies by sociologists of religion). In fact, the relationship of institutional secularisation to secularisation of consciousness is by no means a simple and uniform one and is thus the subject of debates between proponents of secularisation theory and their critics. At best, the position taken at present is that the 'carriers'[1] of secular modes of thought are said to be those educated upper-middle-class groups who dominate the 'knowledge industry' of post-industrial society (the media and educational systems). This group Berger calls a 'cognitive élite' in contemporary society. In the religious realm, it is argued that the clergy and religious are most influenced by the secularising ideas of this élite. The crisis in religious institutions today is a crisis affecting clergy and religious primarily, and, particularly, their younger members. Political and theological liberalism (the result of secularising influences) and anti-institutionalism are the expressions of a crisis of belief among them. Here Daniel Bell's description of the disjunction of culture and social structure is directly relevant.[2] The fundamental tension in society—a tension reflected within the churches—is the disjunction between the traditional values which reinforce the social structure and the culture which has become adversary in its secular values to the traditional modes. This Bell identifies as the crisis of the American Protestant and Catholic churches. This widening gap between large numbers of laity on the one hand, and clergy and institutional spokesmen on the other, was the subject of Jeffrey Hadden's 1969 book, *The Gathering Storm in the Churches*. And while these developments did not happen as dramatically as Hadden predicted, the current view among the sociologists cited, is that the crisis persists.

As to the psychologising tendencies in the churches, a tendency fostered by religious educators and clergy, Daniel Bell has written that the most significant aspect of the current religious crisis is to be found in the search for personal and primordial forms of community. These pursuits, he argues, become substitutes for both traditional religion and for society as well. For at heart they are anti-institutional and set self-experience outside of the moral circle which envelops the total human community. That community links the individual with the past, and in doing so, provides that background (of which Gehlen wrote) from which to derive both a sense of continuity and a sense of obligation.

If the tone of the above analysis is 'debunking', this must be attributed to a regrettable though apparently unavoidable feature of much sociology of knowledge description. In fact, it is not intended that the analysis drive a permanent wedge between traditional religion and modern psychology; rather, it does succeed in illustrating the difficulties involved in their marriage—from the side of religion, one surely not made in heaven. If psychologising threatens religion with increasing secularisation, psychology, at the same time, may be threatened with trivialisation by facile and superficial baptism, as it has in its popular cultural form. Of course, no one seriously thinks that psychology will be affected, in any significant way, by religious co-optation. Nor would it be much affected if religion countered the threat of secularisation by rejecting psychology. On the other hand, it does seem that within the contemporary world religion cannot afford to ignore selected insights offered by psychology, as it cannot afford to develop without taking serious account of itself within the perspectives of contemporary criticism—textual, philosophical, etc. Further, it seems both fair and reasonable to assume that religion's turn to psychology is neither opportunistic nor, in large part, unreflective. Rather, it stems from a need to understand the workings of the mind and to assist the self in living.

The turn to psychology may certainly help to undermine the sense of the universal grounding of one's belief. But have not pluralism and many other elements in the secular culture provided that challenge already? At least, religion, by its turn to psychology—whether ill-fated or not—has asserted its proprietary rights as a long-established tenant of that mind which psychology claims to explore.

Notes

1. The reference is to Max Weber's concept of 'carrier' (*Träger*) meaning the different social strata which were the original bearers of a religion.
2. *The Cultural Contradictions of Capitalism* (New York 1976).

Lee Cormie

Middle Class Spiritualities

1. THE PSYCHOLOGICAL SOCIETY

AMERICAN LIFE is dominated by a cult of the self. Theories and policies are articulated in terms of the discrete, autonomous individual at every level of life and in every domain: personal, interpersonal, political, economic, social and cultural. In a society in which 'science' is the privileged vehicle of truth, the science of psychology offers a wide array of elaborate and refined grammars of the self; and scientifically based psychotherapies offer prescribed ways for the troubled to return to health and normality.

In the period following World War II explicitly psychological perspectives came to play an increasingly influential role within the mainstream Christian churches. Psychology has become a dialogue partner with theology in most seminaries, and pastoral counselling is modelled along the lines of psychotherapy. In the 1960s the churches became important institutional contexts for the profusion of encounter groups, training groups, therapy groups, counselling groups, etc., which were inspired by the new growth psychologies. And in the 1970s religious education programmes for children and adults were shaped in structure and context by psychological models of moral development and faith development. The theory and practice of Christian faith has become thoroughly infused with psychological concepts and sensibilities.

Yet, though little attention has been paid to these findings by psychologists, therapists, doctors, public policy makers and pastoral counsellors who seem to have no room for such findings in their theories, there is strong social scientific support for the claim that personal health and well-being is intimately linked to strategies of capital accumulation fostered by corporate and government leaders. The suicide rate, state mental hospital admission rate, state prison admission rate, homicide rate, cirrhosis of the liver mortality rate, cardiovascular-renal disease mortality rate all correlate most highly with unemployment. It is also clear that these forms of pathology are found more frequently among those with lower incomes.[1] In addition recent studies suggest that at least 30 to 40 per cent of cancers in the general population are caused by industrial pollution.[2]

In other words, the political/economic system in which we live systematically distorts human potential, sickens us, and makes many of us die before our time. How do we explain the persistence of the psychological point of view in the face of this experience and evidence?

2. MIDDLE CLASS SPIRITUALITIES

Throughout its history capitalism has been a dynamic system ever generating conflict and change as corporate owners and managers strive to guarantee higher profits through control over the sources of raw materials, markets, an appropriately trained and disciplined labour force, and government itself. Historically, of course, other groups have struggled against the shifting strategies of capital accumulation, to preserve traditional ways of life, to transform corporate and government policies in their own interests, or sometimes to transform the system itself in the name of justice. These conflicts are always cultural and psychological, as well as political and economic, conflicts involving struggles over the forms of identity, family life and social discipline to be lived out in a society.

The project of forging a national economy and a dominant place in the world system, undertaken by American corporate and political leaders, has been a very violent one. Slaves were forcefully recruited from Africa. Native peoples were eliminated as obstacles to development, either killed or removed to reservations. Immigrants from Europe and China, many of them having been driven off the land by the development of capitalist agriculture and facing starvation, were recruited to work in factories and mines, and on the railroad gangs. Periodic recessions, uneven regional development, and the continued transformation of production kept people on the move within the United States.

Accustomed cultures and forms of subjectivity were continually undermined, along with the institutions that nurtured them. Large scale ideological campaigns by corporate, government and military leaders seeking support for the many wars the United States has waged reinforced this process. Against great odds, given the cultural, racial/ethnic and linguistic differences which separated them (and which were often deliberately aggravated by corporate and political leaders), workers, farmers and women organised themselves to pursue their own interests. None of these movements was completely successful though, and alongside widespread poverty and institutionalised violence there was widespread alienation and all the pathologies associated with it: mental breakdowns, suicides, violent crimes, alcoholism, and marital breakdowns.

By the 1920s the new psychologies, like the psychoanalysis of Freud and the behaviourism of Watson had become influential vehicles of the cult of self; they reflected the tensions and contradictions of American life.[3] In a society where individuals experienced themselves as cut off from others, alone in their struggles to make it in a cruel world, the new psychologies focused on the individual in isolation from institutions and history, and even other people. In a society of huge monopolies and a growing government where the centres of economic and political decision-making were far removed from the lives of most people, the new psychologies reflected a sense of being out of control, under the sway of unconscious or environmental factors. In a society where traditional cultures and patterns of child raising were quickly out of date in terms of the new demands on people, the new psychologies fostered a cult of childhood and critical attitudes towards traditional forms of upbringing. In a society of widespread social conflict and corruption, the new psychologies reflected a certain 'realism' about human nature and human motives, distrustful of reformers and preachers who were interpreted as acting out of repressed sexual and other motives.

But the new psychology was also full of confidence about the ability of people to take control of their own lives, and, with the help of the new therapies, to make of themselves what they wished.

If we interpret the claims to scientific neutrality and certainty as part of the appeal to authority in a society where science is the only form of sacred knowledge, we can see that the new psychologies were manifestations of a new form of secular spirituality for life in an advanced capitalist society. The psychologists were the priests of this new order, formulating and propagating images of human pathology and fulfilment, of sin, grace, and redemption in a troubled society. The therapies were new forms of old rituals of reconciliation seeking to channel the troubled back into the mainstream of life. In this process the psychologists and psychiatrists promoted faith in themselves and the way of life that they advocated, and elicited expressions of faith from the public.

3. PSYCHOLOGY AND IDEOLOGY

No influential spirituality can be understood apart from the economic and political dynamics of life in a society. And this spirituality is no exception. The social struggles over visions and values, theories and practices came to reflect, in the new psychologies, the experience and interests of the dominant actors in this society: upper class, white, males. In this respect the new psychologies reflected the dominant belief in all the social sciences that western capitalist societies represented the highest stage of social, economic, political, and moral evolution, and that the clearest expression of psychic and cultural superiority in these societies was to be found among white men of the upper classes. Women, peoples of colour, poor and working class people generally were interpreted, along with children, as more primitive, as psychically underdeveloped.[4]

The new psychologies did not express the experience and interests of women. Before industrialisation the home had been the centre of production, and women had had a key role to play in helping the family to survive. But the new division of labour split home and work, and in the ensuing struggles to redefine masculinity and feminity, women generally came to be regarded, in the views of the experts, as physically and emotionally inferior to men. Their proper place in life, it was widely asserted, is the home, and their vocation in life is the care of children, who were discovered as fragile creatures needing constant care only in this period, and of husbands, who had to struggle every day out in the cold, hard world of work and politics.

The new psychologies do not reflect the experience and interests of poor and working people. They did not take account of poverty and exploitation, and, by encouraging people to look only within themselves for the sources of their troubles, they actually contributed to their burdens and undermined the thrust towards political responses to them.

The new psychologies also did not reflect the experience and interests of peoples of colour who faced continuing cultural, political, and economic obstacles to survival.

On the other hand, the new psychologies allowed the dominant male *élites* to take their power and success for granted, helped them to confront their troubles, to enjoy the privileges and pleasures that come with success, and to scientifically legitimate their superiority. And the new psychotherapies, by encouraging people to accept their definitions of mental health and mental illness ('madness', neurosis, psychosis), to think about their troubles in these terms, and to think of the therapeutic process or 'cure' as adjustment to these norms, played a very conservative role in promoting the *status quo*; they became subtle instruments of social control.

The new psychologies also provided *élites* with a framework for developing public policies. Welfare and mental health policies were articulated in terms of helping individuals to get back to work. Corporate strategies for increasing productivity were articulated in terms of worker satisfaction. Through elaborate marketing campaigns, corporations were able to continually create new needs which they could then fulfil at great profit even as they left old needs unfulfilled. Increasingly, private life in family and even the secret recesses of the self outside of work and the supermarket, are penetrated by the capitalist agenda: travel, sports, psychotherapy, health, and commercial religions engulf us all. The cult of the self has became a real material force in society, as capitalist development undermines traditional skills and communities and forces people to turn to the market place for goods and services they and their neighbours would have provided for themselves in the past. Advanced capitalism mass produces the forms of personal life.[5] Of course, the majority of Americans at best barely manage to get by from day-to-day. A public policy of expanding indebtedness has enabled some of them to support the economy in the prescribed ways but only at the cost of constant anxiety over an illness or unemployment that will prevent them from paying their bills. Only 20 per cent of American families can afford the affluent life styles celebrated in the media; the rest can only feel inferior.

In the years following World War II the growth or fulfilment psychologies of Allport, Rogers, Maslow and others became very influential. These psychologists manifested a weaker sense of fundamental conflict in the psyche than psychoanalysis and behaviourism; in their writings, it seems, salvation is at hand.

The optimism of these psychologists was widely shared among politicians and social scientists. The United States dominated the world economically, politically, and militarily, and could do no wrong, or so they said. It is the good society itself in operation; anyone who tries hard enough can achieve success and happiness. With enough motivation and discipline Third World countries can in time achieve similar success; there are, in this view, no fundamental conflicts of interest or structural obstacles to achieving the highest stage of development, the society of high mass consumption. This optimism filled the churches too: Christians quickly adopted and blessed the new versions of secular psychological spiritualities. The rejection of positivist methodology by the growth psychologists and their sympathy for religion, in theory and practice, made this conversion easier.

But capitalist development was undermining the grounds for this optimism. The mechanisation of agriculture and mining forced large numbers of rural people, especially Blacks and poor Appalachian Whites, into the cities where there were not enough jobs, houses, schools or public services for them. Economic necessity and the needs for social contacts and outlets for their talents drove many women into the wage labour force. Urban renewal programmes and the policies of banks and insurance companies destroyed neighbourhoods. Management strategies reduced the skills and room for initiative in many formerly attractive jobs. Mechanisation, increasing corporate mobility and a shifting world division of labour meant that many jobs in local communities were lost altogether. Alienation and anomie continue to be widespread, with all the pathological symptoms mentioned above. Those who can afford it are increasingly turning to psychiatrists and psychoanalysts with all the symptoms of narcissism, the endless desperate searching for one's self in a life without meaning.[6]

But some of this frustration and anger was also channelled in political directions by the civil rights/Black power, poor peoples' and feminist movements which exposed the continuing realities of class, racial, and sexual oppression in the United States. By the end of the 1960s the domination of the United States in the world system had been substantially undermined, and there were calls for a new world order as Third World activists revealed the exploitative dynamics at work in the world system, where capitalist modes of 'rational' development produce affluence for a few and poverty, exploitation and oppression for the many, especially for women and peoples of colour.

For a while at least, political, economic and military leaders in the United States have recovered from these attacks on their ideals and policies. With the support of significant numbers of Christians, they have recuperated the ethic of discipline and hard work in the context of the nuclear family with the traditional division of labour and emotion between women and men (as if the economy had not already undermined these forms of life). This harsher, more competitive version of the cult of the self is widely visible in the mass market self-help psychology books.

4. THE PEOPLE OF GOD IN HISTORY

In the Bible God is revealed as a God of love, and we are called to love one another as God has loved us. This love is always personal, but it is not only that, for the loving response of one person to another always takes place in a historical context where there are concrete obstacles to love. So as Christians we are called to respond to the poor person, to the sick and imprisoned, and to nurture communities where human dignity and love can flourish. This is evident in an early baptismal formula: 'Baptised into union with him, you have all put on Christ as a garment. There is no such thing as Jew and Greek, slave and freeman, male and female; for you are all one person in Christ Jesus' (Gal. 3:27-28).

In other words, as Christians we are called to transcend in concrete ways the oppressive divisions that distort individuals and communities: racism/ethnocentrism, class exploitation, and sexism. Of course, efforts to incarnate love and justice, even in small communities, quickly meet with opposition from the guardians of the established order; Christ is crucified again and again in the suffering of the oppressed. So the gift and task of redemption involves a spirituality of resistance to injustice and exploitation, and of active participation in the struggles to transform society. It is in this context, we believe, that we grow and fulfill ourselves, and meet our God.

A new psychology in the service of this project of justice and liberation is already emerging in feminist consciousness-raising groups,[7] in the Black power movement,[8] among activist grass roots communities and movements throughout the Third World.[9] Certainly there is much to learn from mainstream psychologies; and there is no doubt that many psychotherapists have helped their clients, often in spite of their theories, through the compassion and respect they have shown them. Nevertheless, these psychologies and psychotherapies are being fundamentally reconstructed in the process of appropriating them in the projects of liberation.[10]

In the new psychologies that are emerging among these groups there is a clear rejection of positivist claims to neutral, value-free science, in favour of a scientific approach that seeks objectivity through a conscious commitment to the oppressed. This stance involves a critical attitude towards the dominant form of rationality and their scientific legitimations and a clear appreciation of the alternative values, sensibilities and modes of rationality of the cultures of the oppressed, particularly the solidarity, compassion and mutuality that enable them to survive against great odds, and even, on occasion, to be joyful. One of the first tasks of this kind of psychology is, then, the critical recuperation of the cultures of the oppressed.[11]

This kind of psychology involves the analysis of the historical and structural obstacles, often outside the consciousness of individual actors, to integral human development. Thus it is consistently interdisciplinary, seeking to analyse the political/economic/cultural projects of different societies, and the modes of subjectivity and pathology they promote. But it is also liberative, starting from the experience and frames of reference of oppressed people themselves and seeking to identify those places in our everyday lives where we experience our freedom to love and to seek justice.[12]

Finally, these psychologies and psychotherapies are essentially communal projects where each person is respected and supported in her/his efforts to participate as active subjects in changing our history.

People working in these new psychologies do not reduce all psychological problems to political, economic, or cultural problems. Rather, they seek to explore the relationships between the formation of the psyche and the formation of society, to criticise the dominant and often arbitrary definitions of health and madness, and to unfold alternative ways of thinking and acting more humanly. Life and the meaning of life for millions throughout the world are at stake. The irrationality of the dominant rationality of the world system is nowhere more evident than in the willingness of American élites to wage nuclear war to reimpose their order and preserve their privileges in a changing world. Our ability to change our history depends on our ability to link the personal and the social, the theoretical and the practical, faith and politics.

Notes

1. Harvey Brenner *Estimating the Social Costs of National Economic Policy: Implications for Mental and Physical Health, and Criminal Aggression* (Washington: U.S. Government Printing Office, 1976).
2. Samuel S. Epstein *The Politics of Cancer* (Garden City, New York 1979).
3. John Chynoweth Burnham 'The New Psychology: From Narcissism to Social Control' in *Change and Continuity in Twentieth Century America* ed. J. Braeman, R. H. Bremner and D. Brody (Columbus 1968) pp. 351-398.
4. See Louis Dumont *Homo Hierarchicus* trans. M. Sainsbury (Chicago 1970) pp. 1-20; R. T. Hogan and N. T. Elmer 'The Biases in Contemporary Social Psychology' *Social Research* 45 (1978) pp. 478-534; E. V. Sullivan 'A Study of Kohlberg's Structural Theory of Moral Development: a Critique of Liberal Social Science Ideology' *Human Development* 20 (1977) 352-376.
5. See Eli Zaretsky *Capitalism, the Family, and Personal Life* (New York 1976).
6. See R. Sennett *The Fall of Public Man* (New York 1978); C. Lasch *The Culture of Narcissism* (New York 1978); M. Maccoby *The Gamesman* (New York 1978).
7. See Beverly Wildung Harrison 'The New Consciousness of Women: A Socio-Political Resource' *Cross Currents* 25 (1975) 445-461.
8. See D. G. Glasgow *The Black Underclass* (New York 1981), esp. pp. 125-149.
9. See Frantz Fanon *The Wretched of the Earth* trans. C. Farrington (New York 1968); Paulo Freire *Pedagogy of the Oppressed* trans. M. B. Rames (New York 1970); *The Challenge of Basic Christian Communities* ed. Sergio Torres and John Eagleson trans. John Drury (Maryknoll 1981).
10. For an example of appreciative yet critical reconstruction of psychoanalytic theory within a feminist perspective see N. Chodorow *The Reproduction of Mothering* (Berkeley 1978).
11. See Alfredo Moffatt *Psicoterapia del oprimido* (Buenos Aires 1974). I am grateful to Victor Müller of Peru for bringing this excellent work to my attention, and for stimulating discussion about it.
12. I am grateful to Edmund Sullivan of the Ontario Institute for Studies in Education for sharing with me as yet unpublished manuscripts concerning his vision of critical psychology. Also see D. Ingleby 'Understanding "Mental Illness"' in *Critical Psychiatry: The Politics of Mental Health* ed. D. Ingleby (New York 1980) pp. 23-71.

Jarl Dyrud

The Contemporary Debate on 'Narcissism' as a Dominant Cultural Type

IN AMERICA there can be no debate over the fact that our society includes large numbers of people who exhibit self absorption and shallow, unsatisfactory relationships with other people. To a sympathetic listener, they complain of feeling empty of purpose and of living meaningless lives. They seem to exist in a pallid world, not the dead world of the schizophrenic, but an unsubstantial one. There is lively debate over why it happens and what to do about it. Have human beings always been thus and are they only recently noticing it; or is the problem circumstantial in the sense of a response to the contemporary cultural situation? A large literature has developed on both sides of the question.[1]

These selfish, often socially destructive people are now referred to as 'narcissistic'. There have been so many definitions of narcissism put forward in the past two decades however, that the term has lost all specificity and much of its utility. It is fashionable now to speak of 'normal' narcissism as well as pathological narcissism. This dichotomy has been with us at least since the time of the Attic Greeks who observed that man had long struggled with the questions of how it is that self esteem strengthens relationships and thus is good for you, whereas self love weakens relationships and thus is bad for you. It is the latter problem that is addressed in the two earliest written versions of the myth of Narcissus, etymologically the 'numb' one. In both Conon's *Diegeseis* and Ovid's *Metamorphoses* the myth is not a simple story of excessive self-love, but of social impairment. Both versions begin the story with Narcissus rejecting all loving relationships. Underlying aggression is shown in Conon's story in which Narcissus sends a sword to his most persistent lover Ameinias. Ameinias prays to the goddess Nemesis to avenge him, then kills himself with the sword at the door of Narcissus. Subsequently, Narcissus sees his reflection in the pool; he becomes disorganised and dies only when he recognises that it is himself he loves. Ovid emphasised that his recognition led to a fragmentation of himself just as his tears dropping into the still pool disrupted his reflection. The message in both cautionary tales is the folly of rejecting loving relationships. The end is the disruption of the self and the inability to live.

In the intervening years, medieval theologians wrote extensively on the problem of the 'contracted soul' which displayed many characteristics we now call narcissism. From this it seems reasonable to propose that human nature in its intrinsic characteristics has not changed significantly in the past two or three millenia. However, western culture, by which I mean the totality of socially transmitted behaviour patterns, beliefs, and institutions has been evolving toward an ever greater capacity for self-consciousness; which has become, with the discovery of the unconscious, a worried self-distrusting consciousness. This cultural era of widespread self-distrust and self-preoccupation has rightfully been termed 'the era of psychological man'.

There has always been a dynamic tension between human nature and evolving cultural forms which can and do mould it in different ways. The concept of person as moral agent, the subject of his/her verbs, is most attractive to all of us, but such a position must be viewed as an achievement rather than a natural endowment. In the main, we are the unwitting products of our culture. We think and do what is thought and done. It is because of this that reformers have always said in one form or another, 'Wake up! You are asleep in your own lives'.

In the nineteenth century, one distortion of human nature which became prominent was that of hysteria and the obsessive compulsive neuroses. Rational consciousness, as the culture supported it, was being assaulted from underneath by repressed sexual and aggressive drives. Psychoanalysis was developed as a method to broaden our awareness beyond the confines of that particular cultural mould, and gain some semblance of control by a greater knowledge and acceptance of the powerful internal forces that move our lives.

When Sigmund Freud said 'Wake up! Take responsibility for your own life', he never intended to minimise the reality of surprises and disappointments from the outside world. Yet, in seeking to add another dimension by turning the attention inward, he may well have inadvertently set in motion a cultural over-correction that by now in the mid-twentieth century has reduced the 'otherness' and immediacy of experience. Today's psychological man is concerned with gratifying his own needs but pleasure eludes him. Viewing the outer world as a projection of his inner world, he is deprived of response from an 'other'. To the extent that one's relationships with God and man are looked upon as works of a solitary imagination, alienation and anomie, currently included under the term 'narcissism', come to the foreground.

In Freud's time, we had God, conscience, the family, sex, neurotic behaviour and sin all as real issues in a real world. His reality principle set a limit on psychological reality. Now our culture has moved towards replacing sin and conscience with a vague all pervasive sense of guilt, neurotic behaviour with emptiness, sex with alienation, God and the family with a disregard for all authority other than current consensus. It is my impression that this cultural current has made it diffult for psychologically informed clergy to keep from being swept away from issues of sin and redemption into viewing all problems of everyday living as a lack of self-fulfilment. Ellul (1954)[2] observes in this regard that we are now more concerned with what is normal than with what is moral. It is, therefore, not surprising we have come to view narcissism as a clinical problem. Nor is it surprising that psychological man favours inward-looking explanations rather than seeking them in his environment.

In his psychoanalytic psychology Freud described two types of narcissism. He defined primary narcissism the basis of self-esteem, as the investment of the infant's pleasure-seeking drive in the undifferentiated child-mother pair. Good experience in this early period leads to basic trust and increased capacity for later individualisation. Secondary narcissism or self-love could develop only after some separation and individualisation had taken place. This was a psychopathological development in which the pleasure-seeking drive was withdrawn from the frustrating object on to the self, possibly as a defence against aggressive feelings. Freud speculated that a poor experience of primary narcissism leads to vulnerability and a tendency to retreat into secondary narcissism.

Recent infant observations strongly suggest that even newborn babies have some sense of what is me, and not me, that they have relationships as well as impulses. If the infant experiences the 'otherness' of mother much earlier than was previously thought, then the question is whether there ever was a period of primary narcissism without a concurrent object relationship. This lends credence to the early object-relations theorists' work of the past four decades, but does not make verification of their theory any easier.

Freud, with his concern for evidence and proof, concentrated his attention on language and memory. He made some speculations about pre-verbal experience, but did not focus his therapeutic interest on such experience. From his point of view, if there was such early damage it was probably not amenable to psychoanalysis. Melanie Klein, a child therapist, was one of the first psychoanalytic theorists to concentrate on the inner world of pre-verbal experience. Narcissistic issues played a major part in her theory. Her poetic vision provided a mode of expression of the inchoate experience of troubled children and schizophrenics and thus a way of bringing them back to the language of human relationships.

Since Klein, many psychoanalytic writers[3] have tended to describe not only the psychotic and severely character-disordered, but many other kinds of isolated people as 'narcissistic' and worked on a variety of strategies to treat them. The controversy in psychoanalytic thinking centres around the causes of the epidemic of narcissism in our society and breaks roughly into two groups.

The more orthodox group believes that what we are at any stage of our lives—including our level of self-esteem—is the result of the sum total of experiences, some advantageous, some disadvantageous, to which we have been subjected. Self-regard, said Freud, depends on how resilient the ego is, no matter how it got that way. They work more closely with the accessible data—the patient's memories and current evidences of hidden conflict, today frequently secondary narcissistic issues. Thus, the level of inference is lower and the likelihood of confirmation or disconfirmation greater.

The second group, typified by Heinz Kohut and his followers, works on the assumption that unempathic mothering in the earliest months of child care has left a negative imprint—a deficit in primary narcissism. They seek to repair the damaged primary narcissism by an empathic—introspective therapeutic stance. This posture does enhance the patient's self-esteem, but must rely heavily on faith in the analyst's version of what is happening. Theorising has taken on a much more mythical aspect in the hands of the deficit theorists because of its remote relationship to a data base, just as it did with Melanie Klein. The postulated early bad mothering cannot reasonably be verified by the patient because it occurred before the dawn of memory. And, the more orthodox group would add, it is highly unlikely that simple, casual one-to-one relationships exist in the field of human development.

Both psychoanalytic groups share a common concern with the problem of narcissism in our time. As suggested earlier, this particular spiritual hazard of being human has always been part of our nature. Ever since man was able to record his observations, the human race has been struggling with secondary narcissistic issues. The polarity of narcissism versus altruism, alienation versus affiliation, hate versus love has figured prominently in the sacred writings of all major religions. Jesus of Nazareth considered the false self full of pride, and covetousness, an obstacle to the achievement of faith. One had to rid onself of the burden of self-preoccupation before it was possible to have an authentic relationship with God. Psychoanalysis with all of its scientific aura remains in essence another way to attack the heresy of self-love. The Buddhist monk pursuing Satori, the Christian seeking oneness with God, or the psychoanalytic patient working to find a meaningful life, all go through an intense and strenuous activity of self examination. They probe their pride, envy, and malice until they reach an end, often the brink of despair. Then, the false self may recede, effort give way to receptivity and enlightenment, the nothingness of the Buddhist, the presence of God for Christians, the insight of the analysand can take place. From all three perspectives what is presumed to be released is a healthy 'true self' living harmoniously with both an inner and an outer world. For psychological man, enlightenment has become more and more difficult. It is hard to find a place to stand outside solipsism, so the impulse is to look more deeply inward rather than outward.

In response to this impulse, the challenge to faith and theology presented by the deficit theorists is quite different from that presented by the orthodox Freudians. The deficit theory is more like a myth couched in purely psychological terms, a myth that grounds all desire, spiritual and sexual, within the individual's inner world. This form of closure is functionally religious and competitive with other religious explanations. Margaret Mahler[4] (1975) made a statement that could be viewed as the creed of this new religion:

> 'One could regard the entire life cycle as constituting a more or less successful process of distancing from and introjection of the lost symbiotic mother, an eternal longing for the actual or fantasied ideal state of self, with the latter standing for symbiotic fusion with the all-good mother, who was at one time part of the self in a blissful state of well-being.'

Mahler strongly suggests that a self, with itself in an evelope of mother as object, is the goal of all human striving. Not literally returning, but metaphorically reaching the oceanic feeling that Freud described as a product of good mothering. Kohut, the leading advocate of this approach to bliss, emphasises that one does not stay on the mountain top, but returns to daily life having transformed narcissism into empathy, creativity, object love, and wisdom. All the struggles of maturing through resolution of the oedipus complex can be by-passed with this approach. They do not say how it happens, but neither did the long line of religious mystics who experienced oneness with God and were then transformed in their daily lives. Nonetheless, there is a static, hermetic quality to such a psychoanalytically created life purpose that makes primary narcissism a substance of questionable value to fill the centre of life.

The pagan-rationalist psychoanalysts make an effort to strip away illusion so that the patient can find a centre in current human relationships. Paradoxically, they, long thought of as the enemy of religion, made a different and perhaps better preparation for a mature spiritual life. Through the resolution of the oedipus complex, the super-ego becomes a more reliable and benign 'other'—a voice that warns, an eye that watches one's performance. In contrast to some 'ideal state of self' as posed by deficit theory, the parental rival becomes an ideal to emulate in the real world. Guided by the 'otherness' of the super-ego, and the 'otherness' of the ideal, one can prepare a space, not in the centre of one's own person, but at the centre of one's life with other people for an encounter with the 'otherness' of God in a spirit of responsibility and commitment.

Notes

1. See Christopher Lash *The Culture of Narcissism* (Norton 1978), an apocalyptic view, and Paul Zweig *The Heresy of Self Love* (Princeton 1980), a longer view.
2. Jacques Ellul *La Technique* (Paris 1954).

3. Some continuing within Freud's framework of sexual and aggressive drives (the roots of original sin)—first M. Klein, now O. Kernberg; others embracing the Pelagianism of W. R. D. Fairbairn and H. Guntrip (both theologically trained), best represented today by H. Kohut; and finally D. W. Winnicott and M. Mahler, squarely in the middle.

4. M. Mahler, on the first three subphases of the separation-individuation process in *Psychoanalysis and Contemporary Science* 3 ed. L. Goldberger and V. H. Rosen (New York 1975) p. 305.

Brian Mahan

Therapeutic Consciousness and Christian Faith: An American Context

'This above all: to thine own self be true and it doth follow, as night the day, thou canst not then be false to any "man".'

William Shakespeare *Hamlet*: Polonius to Laertes

'What a concord is proposed—between me and my own self: were ever two beings better suited for each other?'[1]

Lionel Trilling to Polonius

I

YEATS, IT appears, finally has his answer: there are now witnesses who claim to offer positive identification of that 'rough beast . . . slouching toward Bethlehem to be born'. It is Narcissus, they say, newly risen from the waters which had claimed him countless centuries before, and last spotted lumbering his way across the American landscape. Like the beast described in the Book of Revelation, Narcissus places his mark on all he claims; and the mark of this beast is 'therapeutic consciousness'. Because the style of selfhood which therapeutic consciousness embodies is one which abhors commitments or loyalties of any description (unless of course it is commitment to the rush of immediate experience or loyalty to a radically truncated vision of self-fulfilment), it is only a matter of time before the vital arteries which link individual identity to social role will be severed and western society destabilised—bled dry. Even now, we are told, though the ponderous machinery of American society drones on for all to hear, it does so only by force of its own mass and momentum, by inertia. It is as if the collective countenance were one of blank resignation or utter boredom. But if our witnesses are to be taken at their word, the gulf which now separates each one from the many may soon give way to the Hobbesian abyss: 'the war of all against all'.

If this were not enough, these same witnesses testify that the emergence of therapeutic consciousness as an anti-heroic cultural ideal threatens to reduce Christian faith to just another technique for inducing and maintaining a sense of psychic balance, distinguished from the rest only by a proclivity for the arcane. We stand warned that if any commitment is more suspect than the response of the citizen to the voice of the collective, it is the response of the believer to the voice of God. One witness describes therapeutic consciousness as an 'anti-religion' and reports that people 'hunger not for personal salvation . . . but for the feeling, the momentary illusion, of personal well-being, health and psychic security'.[2] A second witness pronounced with Zarathustrian flourish that 'the spiritualisers have had their day', and are now involved in devising 'a desperate strategy' aimed at securing acceptance from the high priests of the new therapeutic sensibility.[3] Our culture and our faith have fallen on bad times; or so we have been told.

Hearing all this might give pause even to the most inveterate of theological pluralists: might cause one to wonder whether it may not have been Narcissus's rising from the water which first shook the moorings of traditional American society a decade ago; and whether the accompanying turbulence may have been only initial surface ripples spawned by deep-going, ineluctable tides of cultural change; whether, finally, enthusiasm for change, any change, may have anaesthetised many to the dark possibility that a new epoch of unbelief is already upon us—one in which devotion to any being or cause outside the orbital pull of the Ptolemaic self-system is judged to be symptomatic of immaturity, even inauthenticity.

Still, theologians may not be fully convinced by this testimony. As always, there are others who see things differently. There are those who suggest that the 'light turbulence' which caused the moorings of traditional society 'to give a little' was surely nothing more than the fading wake left by those who ever so briefly attempted to swim against the current. Indeed, it has become fashionable among American journalists to glance back at the political and social upheaval of the late sixties only long enough to document how different things were then from the way things are now. Although scholars are less likely to accept the present moment as the *normans non normata*, many manage, nonetheless, to embrace a similar sentiment: they have come to view that decade as a momentary aberration, as a strange interlude during which the established cultural vision seemed slightly out of focus. Aristides (penname of the editor of *The American Scholar*) observed recently that 'the vaunted greening of America . . . has come to little more than the cropping up of plant shops around the country'.[4] And it does sometimes seem that all that remains are the frills, the window dressing—the ambience of a decade shorn of its substance. After all, the old order did not crumble: traditional power structures remain entrenched; *élite* social and educational institutions again emanate that special aura which sets them apart from the rest; and it is once more possible to be rich and respected at the same time. As for the imminent eclipse of traditional Christian faith, the hand-in-glove relationship between prime-time evangelism and the 'New Right' calls the testimony of Narcissus's accusers into question and gives a measure of credence to the testimony of an earlier witness who had raised the possibility that 'right wing Protestant fundamentalism' may yet provide those who yearn for a relapse into traditional authoritarianism with 'a single orthodox vision of what truth and reality are'.[5]

So enormous is the disparity between the shrill apocalyptic testimony of those who are able to perceive cultural change only in the steady movement of the old order towards the top of the slagheap, and that of the self-assured traditionalists who manage to discern in all manner of unrest and upheaval subtle endorsements for the *status quo*, it is difficult to suppress the suspicion that one side or the other has perjured itself; more difficult still to adopt either vision as a reliable image of the times.

But the tendency of eye witnesses to see the same differently is well known; and this is never more likely than when the witnesses are actors in the scene they describe. Theologian and social scientist alike are susceptible to that myopic distortion of vision induced by staring too intently and for too long at what is too close—too close both emotionally and temporally.

II

The year before Darwin's *The Origin of Species* was published, Louis Aggasiz, then professor of zoology at Harvard, wrote an article in which he defended divine creation of species. Each species was said to represent a single thought in the mind of God; and structural affinities between species were understood as intimations of the process of association of ideas in the Divine Mind, rather than as evidence of common origin, of evolution. Within a decade of the publication of Aggasiz's article, however, New England journals, both popular and scholarly, found themselves enmeshed in the business of determining whether Darwin's developmental theory truly 'substituted blasphemy for the miracle of creation'.[6]

Buoyed by the recent victories over the dual 'irrationalities' of Calvinistic orthodoxy and Emersonian transcendentalism, defenders of the progressive Unitarianism world-vision braced themselves for a prolonged battle. No friend to those who held to the doctrine of Biblical inerrancy, they were unperturbed by the diminished credibility of scriptural accounts of creation resulting from wider acceptance of evolutionary theory. Of greater consequence, however, was the apparent incompatability between descriptions of the tortuously indirect processes by which species were said to evolve and the popularly held, 'quasi-Hegelian' presupposition that nature yielded abundant evidences of the suprarational design of the created universe. Since Darwin's theory described the mechanics of an important aspect of creation without even oblique reference to divine intentionality, questions inevitably arose concerning what evidence might now be proffered in order to provide rational justification for belief. In the hands of the anti-theists these questions were recast into accusations of ontological dishonesty. Although W. C. Clifford's formulation of this accusation ('If a belief has been accepted on insufficient evidence . . . the pleasure is a stolen one. . . . It is wrong always, everywhere, and for everyone to believe anything upon insufficient evidence.'[7]) is perhaps best known, the American historian, John Draper, also stated his case powerfully:

> As to the issue of the coming conflict . . . can anyone doubt. Whatever is resting on fiction and fraud will be overthrown. Institutions that organise impostures and spread delusions must show what right they have to exist . . . mysteries must give place to fact. . . . There must be absolute freedom of thought.[7]

But this harsh rhetoric is misleading. From the very outset of this controversy there were many who, although uncompromising in their conviction that religious belief is duty-bound to provide rational warrants in order to distinguish itself from mere wishful thinking, never judged evolutionary theory to be a threat to the theological project as such. Asa Gray, a botanist and Agassiz's colleague at Harvard, in reviewing an advance copy of Darwin's *The Origin of Species* argued that evolutionary theory was intrinsically neither atheistic or theistic, although it might well be accepted as 'one of the theories of the working of God's plan'. Despite the length of the intervening period during which time theists and atheists exchanged accusations and recriminations, agreeing only that one must choose between Christ and Darwin, by the year 1880 when *The Independent* (the most influential religious newspaper in America at the time) had begun to publish 'full throated polemics on behalf of evolution',[9] Gray's sober analysis had been vindicated. In fact, it is probably safe to say that some thirteen years earlier when Mark

Twain, newly arrived in New York, attended services at prestigious Plymouth Church and witnessed Henry Ward Beecher 'discharging rockets of poetry' and 'exploding mines of eloquence',[10] in the service of his gospel of 'cordial Christian Darwinism', the battle, at least among the educated classes, had already been won. Surely, by the turn of the century when William James wrote that religious beliefs and experiences should be accredited or discredited by assessing their values for life, 'on the whole' and 'over the long run', theistic Darwinism had attained a level of theoretical sophistication unmatched by anything achieved by the Darwinian anti-theists.

It would appear that since the almost tangible sense of apocalyptic urgency which for a time permeated the language of both parties to this nineteenth century controversy was clearly misplaced, we might do well to 'caste a cold eye' upon the present day apocalyptic posturings of those who tell us that 'the centre cannot hold'. Frank Kermode is probably right: 'Crisis is a way of thinking about one's moment and not inherent in the moment itself.'[11] Still, it would be facile to suggest that the contemporary confrontation between therapeutic consciousness and Christianity in America will recapitulate this earlier developmental pattern. It is one thing to conclude that evolutionary theory lends itself to both theistic and atheistic interpretations; quite another to predict that many who today bear the mark of Narcissus will tomorrow collar the yoke of faith.

Indeed, it may be that even stripped of 'last days' rhetoric, the present confrontation between therapeutic consciousness and religious belief is better interpreted as an extension and intensification of the conflict between belief and unbelief during 'the Guilded Age'. There can be little doubt that the individual imaged in this emergent character-type would unhesitatingly grant the anti-theist axiom that 'belief rests upon fraud and fiction'. Oddly, however, by rejecting what had formerly been judged a self-evident corrolary to this axiom (that the greatest danger posed to individual autonomy by religion was the believer's inevitable abnegation of the responsibility to affirm only those propositions supported by sufficient evidence) the way was cleared for a radical escalation of the anti-theist offensive in the twentieth century.

In therapeutic consciousness the freedoms most prized are many: the freedom to respond without inhibition to the urgings of impulse, the freedom to focus uninterruptedly upon the present moment, the freedom to discover the true self hidden beneath the social mask, and so on; but the overarching freedom which unites these lesser freedoms is no longer Draper's 'absolute freedom of thought', but the absolute freedom to exercise personal control over one's interior life—all of it, not only its cognitive aspect. Because of this, those who bear the mark of Narcissus expend little energy attempting to refute the propositional truths affirmed by the believer. Their concern now is with religion's claim to truth as a way of life, 'as a pattern of being in relation to others and to God',[12] as faith. Convinced that religion functions mainly to legitimate a restrictive, anti-instinctual social order, one which is always poised to usurp control of the internal processes which organise experience, therapeutic consciousness perceives faith's promise of salvation (even when this promise has reference to the transformation of life before death) as a threat to its autonomy.

But, it is not as difficult a matter to turn one's back to the promise of salvation as it once was. Well tutored in the use of the various 'techniques of selfhood' associated with popular distillations of psychoanalytic theory and technique, modern consciousness increasingly is empowered to maintain an attitude of studied indifference before faith's once enticing blandishments. For this reason, the new manifesto issuing from the spiritual scions of Freud is at one and the same time less confrontational and more thoroughgoing than that of the anti-theists.

> Throw away all the old keys to the great riddles of life; depth in psychology brings 'men's' minds around from such simplifications to an active resignation in matters

such as they are to a modest hope, and to satisfiable desires.[13]

No longer intent upon challenging religion's right to exist, therapeutic consciousness wishes only to be left alone to tend the garden of its own interiority.

III

For the stalwart believer, as unpleasant as it is to be misunderstood, slandered or berated, such indignities can usually be borne with equanimity; on occasion they may even be interpreted as signs of favoured status. But to be ignored, to have one's testimony ruled out of order, declared irrelevant, struck from the record: this is unbearable. In therapeutic consciousness it appears that faith has found an adversary it never expected to encounter: a wide-eyed, self-proclaimed subscriber to the ethic of 'invincible ignorance'. How can the promise of salvation ever reach one who does not have ears to hear and whose eyes 'are endlessly looking inside for some sense of fulfilment as if it were some vast warehouse of gratification'.[14] It is difficult to imagine an environment less hospitable to the life of faith than this.

But according to one Catholic theologian there is a worse-yet beyond this bad-enough. James Hitchcock contends that since Vatican II American Catholics have adopted the 'therapeutic mentality' 'without even realising it'. So complete is the capitulation of traditional faith that we may be in imminent danger of finding 'the God of Abraham, Isaac and Jacob replaced by the God of Sister Corita, Rod McKuen and Jonathan Livingston Seagull'. Anxious to prevent this, Hitchcock cautions his fellow believers that 'personal experience . . . will always exercise a disproportionate influence and hence is always in need of amplification and corrections from some source outside itself'. 'True Christians,' he goes on to say, 'believe in the teachings of Christ, not their own experience.'[15]

Surely this is a harsh disjunction, but not an entirely unexpected one given the fact that Hitchcock's analysis is heavily dependent upon the religio-cultural observations of Philip Rieff, one of the earliest and easily the most ingenious of Narcissus's accusers. Similar denigrations of personal experience as legitimate arbiter of meaning and value, inspired in part by Christopher Lasch's popularisation of the notion of 'the culture of narcissism', have begun to appear with some frequency in popular American periodicals, including liberal Christian publications like *The Christian Century*.[16]

But not everyone agrees that the psychic boundaries which separate Christian faith from therapeutic consciousness can be so easily demarcated. Sensitive to the moralistic connotations of the myth of Narcissus, the psychiatrist and student of culture, Robert Jay Lifton has chosen Proteus as the mythic standard bearer for his own model of therapeutic consciousness.[17] This model resembles those of Rieff and Lasch in that the personality-type it describes is suspicious of any call to commitment which threatens to disrupt the smooth functioning of the internal processes which sponsor and protect the feelings of psychic wholeness and balance; it differs from them, however, in that this suspicion is not unequivocal. Plagued by a vague but persistent sense of guilt and a nagging feeling of unworthiness, the individual Lifton describes has begun to search, however haltingly, for perduring values which can sustain life even in the face of death.

Sadly, it is beginning to appear that we latter day defenders of Christian faith in America are no more disposed to welcome the moderating influence of Lifton and his life than were our predecessors to welcome that of Asa Gray. Despite our protests to the contrary, we seem little moved by the news that those who bear the mark of Narcissus have emerged from their 'vast warehouse of gratification' to seek an answer to the question of meaning of life. And the reason for this is as plain as it is disheartening: their search has not led them where we had hoped it might—to us.

Rebuffed, feeling ourselves misunderstood, we instinctively shy away from speaking of our faith experientially. Adopting a tone of moral indignation, we castigate those who have ratified the new anti-theist manifesto, telling them that they have wed themselves to a vision of human destiny so narrowed, so self-enclosed that it is incapable of further diminishment. Although we are uneasy about alarmist tactics employed by the accusers of Narcissus, by and large we now accept their testimony; we respond to their tocsin call and prepare ourselves to defend our faith and our society. And so we have begun to draw the battle-lines: faith to the one side—serene, willing to serve; unbelief to the other—distracted, prideful.

Having denied the ambiguity of therapeutic consciousness, we need not accept the ambiguity of our own faith as experienced. More particularly, in discounting the suspicion of our adversaries that the language of belief often obscures the fact that our dependency on God may stifle the sense of autonomy essential for true integrity of character, we divert our attention from the terrible ambiguity of Christian self-sacrifice: 'Self-sacrifice may be worthless, if there is no self worthy of being sacrificed.'[18]

Perhaps the most bitter irony of our situation is that in fleeing from the ambiguity of our faith as experienced, we forfeit whatever moral authority we might have claimed. As Josef Pieper says, it is only 'the hidden abandonment' of self to God, manifest in 'the unconditional acceptance of insecurity', which distinguishes the capacity for true moral discernment from 'the noisy sterility of spiritual pride'.[19] Less ironically, but more tellingly, we may also have missed our opportunity to speak humanly and convincingly to those who search for a deeper fulfilment than the kind engendered by proficient application of the 'technologies of selfhood'. Fearful of ridicule, still bristling from our rejection, we cannot risk the vulnerability required of self-revelation. Once more, we moralise. We offer salt water to those who have begun to thirst for the 'water which wells up to eternal life' and substitute accusation and guilt for 'the radical peace the world cannot give'.[20]

Again: to embrace the ambiguity of faith as experienced is not to relinquish our claim to moral authority. Quite the contrary, it signals the efficacious presence of co-operative grace, the immanent, enabling principle of Christian life, and the prerequisite of authentic fortitude. Finding ourselves forgiven and loved without condition, we are empowered, we are coerced 'to recall the sins of self and to confess what the self shudders to remember'.[21] And there is much to remember. For one thing, we believers—with few exceptions—never fully give up on our attempts to heal ourselves. We differ from those who bear the mark of Narcissus only in that with each fresh failure we come closer to understanding the folly of our attempts. Thus, when we speak sternly to others of their folly, we should do so only after first enjoying a good laugh at our own expense. How was it that we came to believe we could be one with ourselves without first being reconciled to our God: 'What a concord is proposed—between me and my own self: were ever two beings better suited for each other?'

Notes

1. Lionel Trilling *Sincerity and Authenticity* (Cambridge, Ma. 1972) pp. 3-4.
2. Christopher Lasch *The Culture of Narcissism* (New York 1979) p. 33.
3. Philip Rieff *The Triumph of the Therapeutic* (New York 1966) p. 18.
4. Joseph Epstein *Familiar Territory* (New York 1979) pp. 42-55.
5. See Robert Bellah *New Religious Consciousness and the Crisis of Modernity* (Berkeley 1971) pp. 350-351.

6. See Bruce Kuklick *The Rise of American Philosophy; Cambridge, Ma., 1860-1930* (New Haven 1977) pp. 21-24.

7. From Morton White *Science and Sentiment in America* (London 1972) pp. 188-189.

8. From Shaw Persons *Free Religion: An American Faith* (New Haven 1947) pp. 100-101.

9. See Richard Hofstadter *Social Darwinism in American Thought* (Boston 1944) pp. 13-30.

10. See Justin Kaplan *Mr Clements and Mark Twain* (New York 1966) chap. 1.

11. Frank Kermode *The Sense of an Ending: Studies in the Theory of Fiction* (London 1966) p. 101.

12. James Fowler *Stages of Faith* (New York 1981) p. 295.

13. Rieff p. 40.

14. Richard Sennett *Authority* (New York 1980) p. 117.

15. James Hitchcock *Catholicism and Modernity: Confrontation or Capitulation* (New York 1979) p. 47.

16. See, for example, Janet Karsten Larson 'The Rhetoric of Narcissism' in *The Christian Century* 98 No. 27 (7 September 1981).

17. See Robert Jay Lifton *The Broken Connection* (New York 1979) pp. 29, 296-297.

18. See Josef Pieper *The Four Cardinal Virtues* (Notre Dame 1966) pp. 140-141.

19. Paul Tillich *Systematic Theology* (Chicago 1967) vol. 3, pp. 43-44.

20. Bernard Lonergan's phrase. See Bernard Lonergran *Method In Theology* (New York 1972) p. 105.

21. H. Richard Niebuhr *The Meaning of Revelation* (New York 1960) pp. 83-84.

Bulletins

Judith van Herik

The Feminist Critique of Classical Psychoanalysis

THERE HAS been no one unified feminist critique of classical psychoanalysis, which I here define as texts written by Freud. Some feminist questions have been addressed primarily to those of his papers which explicitly discuss the psychology of women, female sexuality, and femininity. There are only three of these and all were relatively late: 1925, 1931 and 1933.[1] The questions asked most often of these works are: are their claims about women's psychology correct? If they are not, how and why are they not? And, what are the consequences for women of Freud's errors? Feminist questions have also been asked of the whole of Freud's psychoanalytic corpus, about its complex and variously interpreted messages about human nature and culture. This is for the most part a more recent endeavour. On the one hand, Freudian theory as a whole has been seen as an influential example of sexist theory, so that Freud is taken as an important contemporary enforcer of sexism. On the other hand, in a move that some may consider paradoxical, the Freudian texts have been understood as a resource for feminist analysis, as material with which to design a feminist remedy for sexist culture as a whole. Those who see Freud as prototypical sexist ask: what are the defining characteristics of sexist theory? And where are these characteristics found in Freud's writings? Here, everything which assays his mind, including his letters and personal life, is relevant data. Those who want to use Freudian theory for feminist construction ask: how does Freudian psychoanalytic theory account for systematic, apparently universal, sexism? How is this account useful for a feminist analysis of the problem? And, what programme for change does this analysis suggest? Here, data is not his personal views or conduct, but the logic of his theory.

Scholars who did not identify themselves as feminists have contributed to feminist critiques, as I define 'feminist'. (For example, Simone de Beauvoir did not consider herself such when she wrote *The Second Sex* [*Le Deuxième Sexe*, 1949], she now does.) My definition of 'feminist' has a more scholarly than political emphasis. It means deriving one's questions from the insight that the sexes have been and are considered to be of asymmetrical value, and treating this as the problem rather than as an unexamined presupposition. De Beauvoir's analysis of man as prototypical human subject, while woman is 'other', is thus a classical statement of this insight. By this definition, a feminist critique is not interested just in sex or gender difference, but in the asymmetrical evaluation of supposed differences. (Sex is bio-anatomical; gender is psycho-social.

Feminist theorists tend to argue that gender is contingent and humanly produced.) From this point of view, to assume that the sexes are opposite but complementary (symmetrical) misses the feminist point: that the assumed differences are consistently disadvantageous to females, whether or not females are 'feminine'. Further, an asymmetrical conception of the genders entails three assumptions: masculinity is the general human norm, femininity a special case; the point of view assumed is a masculine one and it *looks at* the feminine; and the masculine is, actually or potentially, of greater value, it alone is capable of expressing the human ideal.[2] Freud's theory relies upon these assumptions; it is a gender-asymmetrical theory. What differentiates those who realise this and therefore reject Freudian psychology as harmful to women from those who realise this but use Freudian theory for feminist purposes is that the latter judge Freud to have created a theory *about* gender asymmetry as well as a gender-asymmetrical theory. For them, Freud shows how gender is humanly produced.

Here, I sketch positions of (1) those who criticise Freudian psychology of women to revise or reject it; (2) those who criticise the whole of Freudian thought as sexist; and (3) those who wish to use Freudian theory in service of feminist goals. I then comment on (4) the relevance of feminist critiques of Freud for 'dialogue' between theology and Freud.

1. THE CRITICISM OF FREUD'S PSYCHOLOGY OF WOMEN

Prior to 1925, Freud's formal psychology of women was largely an appendix to (male) oedipal theory. If the oedipal boy loved his mother in rivalry with his father then the girl's problem was the mirror image of his. So Freud assumed that girls' first love-objects were fathers. After 1925, Freud claimed that girls also first loved mothers, so that achieving an Oedipus complex meant 'changing their sex' from a masculine, clitoral focus to a feminine (vaginal) one and their love-object from the mother to the father. The preoedipal mother-love was repressed, he thought, because of disappointment about being 'castrated' like the mother. This was the source of unconscious 'penis envy'. Becoming psychologically feminine entailed accepting 'castration', passivity and the status of object of the father-subject's love. In different ways, Freud traced feminine character to this presumed buried sequence of events. Its characteristics included inclinations to masochism, envy, intellectual inferiority, hysteria and narcissism; and hostility to culture. Criticism of this account began immediately. Until the mid-1930s, papers by Ernest Jones, Karen Horney, and others argued that girls had primary, natural, feminine libidinal desires. (For Freud, libido was by definition masculine, because it was active.) For Freud's critics, to say that femininity is achieved in a tortuous infantile development was to see women as a secondary rather than a primary sex. Horney believed that Freud's errors derived from viewing women from a male's—actually, a phallic-stage boy's—point of view, from treating castration as a physical fact, and from mistaking penis envy for a result of anatomy when its source was awareness of males' cultural advantages. For Horney, Freud was blind to symmetry and missed, for example, male envy of the womb. More recent criticisms often draw on Horney. Their programme has been empirical as well as theoretical, and has focused on disproving the distinction between clitoral and vaginal orgasm and the occurrence of, or Freudian explanation for, penis envy.[3]

2. THE CRITICISM OF FREUD'S PSYCHOLOGY AS A WHOLE

Criticism of Freud's psychology of women uses and contributes to criticism of Freud's entire theoretical edifice as sexist. Much of this literature has been American, probably because in the USA by the 1950s and '60s much of the popular and professional idiom about 'normality' and neurosis was vaguely Freudian. Americans developed a species of Freudian thought that emphasised social conformity as a therapeutic goal and was more didactic, moralistic, popular, optimistic and environmentalistic than Freud.[4] In its approach to femininity, it was also more biologically deterministic. Whether neo-Freudian or 'orthodox', the popular American view of the psychology of women came to be that the healthy, happy and moral woman selflessly submitted to biology, to husband, and to domestic demands. De Beauvoir's discussion of Freudian bad faith about women in *The Second Sex* reinforced overemphasis on biological determinism in Freud's psychology of women.

Some American women had responded with enthusiasm, in the teens and twenties, to what they understood to be the Freudian message (that women, too, have legitimate sexual needs) because of its criticism of 'Puritan' mores. By the 1960s, this response was forgotten. Between 1963, which saw the publication of Betty Friedan's *The Feminine Mystique*, and in 1970, when Kate Millet published *Sexual Politics*, numerous feminist critics treated psychoanalysis as a male-centred ideology that served men's interests and sexist society by recommending the false consciousness of adjustment to feminine roles and that placed women in a 'double bind'.[5] On one level, women were praised for accepting femininity; at another, they were told that it was an inadequate human stance. If a woman rejected femininity she was neurotic; if she accepted it, she was not successfully human. This kind of criticism is important for feminism, but it responds to the hegemony of a revised Freud in the USA as much as to the Freudian texts themselves.

3. THE USE OF FREUDIAN THEORY IN THE SERVICE OF FEMINIST GOALS

Several significant studies have found Freudian methods and insights useful for analysing sexism with a view to overcoming it. While no one claims that this was Freud's programme, exposure of Freudian thought as ideology has been followed by use of its understanding of unconscious processes and of oedipally-formed gender to explain the tenacity of that very asymmetrical ideology. By making careful distinction between (*a*) Freud's descriptive analysis of the feminine situation and his prescription of it and (*b*) between sex and gender, and by taking seriously Freud's views on the transgenerational power of unconscious processes to reproduce gender asymmetry, such analysts have found in Freud suggestions about how to cut the knot of asymmetry in its unconscious roots. Their recommendations differ, but in this category belong Shulamith Firestone's *The Dialectic of Sex* (1970), Juliet Mitchell's *Psychoanalysis and Feminism* (1974), Dorothy Dinnerstein's *The Mermaid and the Minotaur: Sexual Arrangements and Human Malaise* (1976), Helen Block Lewis's *Psychic War in Men and Women* (1976) and Nancy Chodorow's *The Reproduction of Mothering: Psychoanalysis and the Sociology of Gender* (1978). In France, essays by Hélène Cixous and Luce Irigaray's *Speculum de l'autre femme* (1974) and *Ce sexe qui n'en est pas un* (1977) have been important. Mitchell's central claim is well known: that Freud provides an analysis of unconscious mental life in patricentric culture and that adequate strategies for change should be based on this analysis.

Freud has been read differently by feminists who reject and who use his theories. To oversimplify, the former understand him as a *psychologist* (of women); the latter, as a *theorist of* (gender-asymmetrical) *culture*. Students with theological interest have also read him variously. Again to oversimplify, some have rejected him as a psychologist (of religion), often stressing his diagnosis of Christian ideas as wish-fulfilling illusions. Some have read him as a theorist of culture to ask what this theory has to say to theology.[6] But theological use of Freud's analysis of culture as *gender-asymmetrical* has just begun. If theologians can use feminist criticism of Freud in their dialogue with his thought, those who make that use may ask: what if, descriptively, gender asymmetry has been assumed in our theologies, but, prescriptively, should not be? If one draws from Freud the hypothesis that the conviction of the inevitability of gender asymmetry is itself a wish-fulfilling illusion, what theological revisions must follow? In short, Freud, as read by some feminist critics, challenges patricentric and gender-asymmetrical theological assumptions.

Notes

1. Sigmund Freud 'Some Psychical Consequences of the Anatomical Distinction between the Sexes' *The Standard Edition of the Complete Psychological Works of Sigmund Freud* ed. James Strachey (London 1953-1974) XIX pp. 248-258 ('Einige psychische Folgen des anatomischen Geschlechtsunterschieds' *Gesammelte Werke* [London 1940-] XIV pp. 19-30); 'Female Sexuality' *SE* XXI pp. 225-243 ('Über die weibliche Sexualität' *GW* XII pp. 517-537); 'Femininity' *SE* XXII pp. 112-135 (in *Neue Folge der Vorlesunge zur Einfuhrung in die Psychoanalyse GW* XV).

2. See chap. 2 of my *Freud on Femininity and Faith* (Berkeley, Los Angeles and London 1981).

3. For citation and discussion of early criticism, see Zenia Odes Fliegel 'Feminine Psychosexual Development in Freudian Theory: A Historical Reconstruction' *Psychoanalytic Quarterly* 42 No. 3 (1973) pp. 385-408. For recent criticism, see Julia A. Sherman *On the Psychology of Women: A Survey of Empirical Studies* (Springfield, Ill. 1971) chaps. 3 and 4.

4. See Nathan G. Hale, Jr. *Freud and the Americans: The Beginnings of Psychoanalysis in the United States, 1876-1917* (New York 1971) chap. 13.

5. Gregory Bateson, *et al.* 'Toward a Theory of Schizophrenia' *Behavioural Science* 1 No. 4 (1956) 251-264.

6. E.g., Peter Homans *Theology After Freud: An Interpretive Inquiry* (New York and Indianapolis 1970); Paul Ricoeur *Freud and Philosophy: An Essay on Interpretation*, trans. D. Savage (New Haven 1970).

James Fowler

Theology and Psychology in the Study of Faith Development

IN THIS volume, devoted to psychology's challenge to faith, it is my responsibility to report briefly on research and theory construction which have engaged me and my associates since 1972. This work, designated as faith development theory, focuses at an intersection of theology and developmental psychology, in an effort to illumine our understanding of the formation and transformation of lived faith. The developmental psychologies we draw upon come from two principal families of theories. On the one hand, we draw upon the psycho-social approaches of Erik Erikson, Daniel Levinson, and others. Behind these life-cycle theorists lie the psycho-sexual constructions of Freud. Our work and Levinson's depend also to a degree on C. G. Jung's reflections on the individuation process. On the other hand, we have been fundamentally influenced by the developmental structuralism of Jean Piaget, in the cognitive domain, and of Lawrence Kohlberg in the area of development of moral reasoning. Behind these figures lie John Dewey and J. Mark Baldwin, and ultimately, of course, Immanuel Kant.

Both the life-cycle theorists and the structural developmentalists offer philosophical psychologies. Particularly in relation to Piaget and Kohlberg one can ask whether the work is really psychology at all. Piaget described his own discipline as genetic epistemology; Kohlberg's might well be described as genetic ethics. In both cases there is an effort, through empirical inquiry and philosophical construction, to identify evolving patterns of thought resulting from the construction and integration of cognitive operations in a sequence of stage-like systems. Our work might be designated as genetic theology, or perhaps genetic *pisteuology* (Gr. *pisteuo*, 'I believe', or better, 'I rest my heart, I give my full devotion'). Our study focuses on persons, interacting with communities of shared meaning and in the force-fields of our lives, as we compose guiding images of the ultimate conditions of existence, and shape our lives in relation to the character of value and power in the ultimate, and to the neighbour and the mundane world, in light of that which has or is ultimacy for us. Faith, so understood, is usually religious faith. But it need not be. Images of ultimacy in our lives may centre in causes, persons, or goals that promise to give our lives meaning, security, or nobility. These centres of value and power may take on 'god-value' for us, becoming axes around which our lives and their meanings rotate, but they, and our relation to them, are not necessarily religious.

Our project, then, has involved the effort to understand and clarify a sequence of developmentally related stage-like styles of being in faith. Employing the notion of faith sketched in the last paragraph, we have asked whether, paralleling qualitative stages in cognitive and moral reasoning operations, there are not stages of faith — integrated operations of knowing and valuing by which persons compose their images of an ultimate environment and commit themselves to, and guide their everyday lives in relation to, the character of value and power it discloses. From Piaget and Kohlberg we retain the commitment to formalism — to describing stages of faith by reference to the operations or *ways* of making and maintaining meaning, rather than with regard to the *contents* or the *substance* of faith. Our interviews do enable a person to disclose his or her theology or world view. Our interest, in addition, however, is to identify the operations of knowing and valuing *by which* that theology or world view is composed. We want to discern the structuring of the self-ultimate-other relation from which a person's faith arises.

From the life-cycle theorists (Erikson, Levinson, *et al.*) we have retained an interest in life history and in systematic reflection on the predictable challenges and turning points in psycho-social maturation. We are interested in understanding how experiences and relationships at any point in the life-cycle affect both the content and the structuring of a person's faith. We are critically interested in how and why transition from one structural stage to another occurs in the life-cycle. Space does not permit us here to explore the implications of relating an understanding of structural stages to the phases or seasons of the life-cycle perspectives. Perhaps it is sufficient to suggest that a so-called 'midlife transition' may be construed and dealt with in quite different ways by a person best described in structural terms by the Synthetic-Conventional stage of faith and by one whose stage is Individuative-Reflective.

Theologically, the most decisive influence on faith development studies has been H. Richard Niebuhr. In the context of his central conviction of God's priority in being, value, and power, which he expresses in terms of the sovereignty of God, Niebuhr's theology undertakes a powerful description of the human life of faith. In a method I have elsewhere called 'confessional phenomenology', Niebuhr invites us to attend to the dynamics of human faith, formed and maintained in triadic relations, in which our human trusts and loyalties are deepened and grounded in shared commitments to centres of value and power which transcend us. Niebuhr's transformationist theology depicts the conversion, by a succession of revolutions in our life of faith, from the polytheism of many value centres and diffuse faith, through the henotheism of idolatry, and on to radical monotheistic faith in one God, in relation to whom all else finds its proper, relative value. Parallels between this movement in Niebuhr's theology and similar movements towards universalising justice in Kohlberg, and towards inclusive species identity in Erikson, should be noted. Together these parallel the developmental movement traced in stages of faith.

Since 1972 we have interviewed 359 persons, from ages four to ninety. This group is virtually equally divided between males and females and includes Protestants, Catholics, and Jews, as well as some agnostics and atheists. With minor exceptions they are all North American. In this cross-sectional data, gathered by way of semi-clinical interviews, we have found, after infancy, six distinctive stage-like styles of making and maintaining meaning; stages in the composing and articulation of faith.

These stages are more fully described in other writings and can only be briefly sketched here:

Undifferentiated Faith: The pre-linguistic, largely pre-conceptual forming of the infant's disposition towards an environment gradually recognised as distinct from the self. In pre-images that precipitate out of the quality of the child's interaction with primary caregivers and her/his organismic hope, trust in the environment and in the meanings embodied in parental care support a sense of self as worthy, cherished, and at home.

Intuitive-Projective Faith: Typically forming between ages two and six, this stage involves the acquisition of language and the awakening of imagination. In the absence of cognitive operations allowing for reversibility of thought and the testing of perceptions, the child grasps experience in powerful images. Attentive to the gestures, rituals, and words adults use in their language of faith, the child's capacity for attention to mystery and the numinous can be focused and formed by her or his perceptions of the adults' faith and convictions.

Mythic-Literal Faith: Taking form usually between ages seven and twelve, this stage marks children's abilities to question their images of faith, testing them in accordance with the teachings of valued adults and with their own more developed capacities for reversing their thoughts and testing their perceptions. With new capacities for perspective-taking overcoming the ego-centrism of the previous stage, and with a firm grasp of cause-effect relations, children in this stage begin to form and grasp their meanings by way of narrative or story.

Synthetic-Conventional Faith: Beginning around twelve another revolution in meaning-making occurs for most youth. New cognitive abilities (early formal operations) make it possible for the youth to begin to construct the image of self he/she believes significant others hold. ('I see you seeing me; I see the me I think you see.') This liberation from embeddedness in one's experience of self gives rise to a struggle to synthesize an identity—some livable unity of the 'me's I think they see'. It also raises the possibility and necessity of reflecting on the meaning of one's stories. In the previous stage the child *is* his stories. In this stage it emerges that the young person *has* stories. Having stories means asking, what do they mean? With the synthesis of identity there is a corresponding readiness for synthesis of meanings to support and guide the newly self-conscious self. This is a con-forming stage (forming the self in reliance with and upon others). It locates authority between the 'others' and the forming self. Many adults continue in this stage of faith well beyond adolescence or young adulthood.

Individuative-Reflective Faith: Around twenty, and not much younger, some persons begin a transition from the previous stage to one in which self-reflection is no longer so dependent upon others, but upon the emergence of a capacity for dialogue between the selves others see and a self 'accessible only to me'. Questions of authentic selfhood come to the fore, and with them, questions regarding the truth of the values and outlook one holds. Employing full formal operational thinking, this stage takes on the burden of choice and exclusion of options in faith. Authority, previously located externally, must now be located in the self. Not individualistic, in this stage membership in communities is chosen or reaffirmed rather than being merely a matter of inheritance.

Conjunctive Faith: In some adults, usually after age thirty-five, the clear boundaries of self and outlook constructed by the previous stage begin to blur. Images of the self formed in young adulthood demand to be revised. New attention to polarities and ambiguities in the self and in life call for recognition. Paradoxes, and the unity of opposites in efforts to grasp truth begin to be attractive. Usually a reworking and reclaiming of earlier truths from childhood must be undertaken, and there is both interest in and readiness to learn from traditions of truth previously experienced as foreign to one's own. This stage represents a critical step in the relativisation of self as central in meaning-making, and towards a complementarity with being in which a more radical caring for others is possible.

Universalising Faith: A rare stage, the persons who are best described here may be said to have relinquished self as the axis for faith knowing and to have found self more fully as part of the commonwealth of being to which their loyalty is committed. By virtue of their love of being and their genuine, unforced self-transcendence, we experience them as revolutionary in their perspectives and their care. Inclusive visions, subordinating entrenched interests to the fulfilment of being, enables them to unmask our parochial idols and to call us, by teaching or quiet example, to righteousness and to wider, less self- or group-centred faith.

Space does not permit a proper discussion either of the dynamics of stage transition or of conversion. Conversion, a gradual or sudden alteration in the *contents* of faith (centres of value, images of power, one's master stories) may or may not involve stage transition.

CONCLUSION

In faith development theory theology and psychology are asked to work together in the investigation and illumination of the dynamics of faith. Empirical investigation plays the critical role of testing, refining, or replacing theological and/or psycho-philosophical constructions. Finally, psychological constructions are subjected to theological control in this work, but in a way which intends to avoid both reducing their critical and constructive contributions to theology or subordinating them to doctrinal strictures. Within the conviction of the sovereignty of God, faith development theory employs theology, empirical inquiry and psychological theory in a way intended to enable them to contribute in partnership to the understanding and illumination of the humanward side of the dynamics of faith.

Wolfgang Bartholomäus

New Theories in the Adlerian School

ANYONE WISHING to state the challenge posed to the Church and religious belief by Individual Psychology is faced with a specific difficulty. Through his break with Freud due to the emergence of new ideas, Adler introduced the principle of 'further development' (Ringel 1978, 149) into psychoanalysis in 1911. It took a long time for this principle to bear any fruit in Individual Psychology. A taboo subject in psychoanalytic circles, banned by the National Socialists and forgotten by the (second) post-war generation, Individual Psychology has since 1970 attempted to find its own identity. This it has done by revitalising its history, primarily the works of Adler, and by setting up a dialogue with other schools of psychology. In doing so, there proved to be more common ground than had been expected. Individual Psychology described this course of events (Kausen 1977a), approved the 'convergence of principles of depth psychology' hoped for by Birnbaum (Birnbaum 1948, Ringel 1973, 1978a), emphasised its readiness to listen to all sides (Ringel 1978a), showed its relationship to other theories and therapies (psychoanalysis, ego-psychology, humanistic psychology and behavioural therapy) (Kausen 1977c, Spiel 1978, Antoch 1979, Seidenfuss 1981), and registered its partial acceptance by other sciences (ethology, motivation research, gestalt psychology, social psychology and sociology (Kausen 1977c)). As a result, there was spectacular progress in Individual Psychology more in the direction of reciprocal assimilation of twentieth century psychology or a 'further development in new forms' (Kausen 1977c, 915). A brief mention of this would include ego-psychology, narcissism and interaction theory among others. In any case, the details of Individual Psychology theory were also made more comprehensible and precise, and here I should only like to discuss the details briefly within the framework of the anthropology of Individual Psychology. It can be understood under the following headings: wholeness (*Ganzheit*), sociability (*Sozialität*), activity, finality and self-assurance (*Selbstsicherung*).

Individual Psychology did not accept the Freudian interest in the structure of the mechanism of the psyche, although it lends itself to a full explanation of the wholeness of man. The following belongs to its diachronic aspect: the unconscious and the conscious, the id, the ego and the superego should not be seen as opposing one another (Titze 1979) and yet a possible conflict 'has a valuable place in [man's: W.B.] individual lifestyle, and finds its meaning and reaches its goal there' (Antoch 1980b, 118. 1980a). The following belongs to the synchronic aspect: the whole man is comprised of body and soul (as opposed to the narrowness of biologism), mind and body (as opposed to the one-sided spiritualist view) and of physical nature (*Physis*) and metaphysical nature (*Metaphysis*) (as opposed to the immoventist misunderstanding). A 'universal image of man' (Ringel 1981, 46) which goes so far as to take account of the metaphysical-religious dimension of man, can justifiably be said to belong to the theory of Individual Psychology as Adler was open to the concept of God (Adler 1933a, 1933b. Metzger 1979). Individual Psychology attempts to incorporate this in its therapy.

The whole man (the in-dividual) needs to communicate with his fellow-men, and the theory of man as being primarily a social being has been corroborated many times (Kausen 1977b). Individual Psychology has carried out more in-depth research into man's need to belong and to participate, which in its purest form was dubbed 'a sense of community' by Adler. This is not the same thing as conformity. Adler had already made the distinction between the real society and the ideal community, and had used the utopian forms of the ideal community as his criteria for criticising the truth of the real society (Spiel 1948). 'A sense of community' also does not mean shying away from conflict or even a total avoidance of conflict, but 'should be understood in the sense of being basically disposed towards close contact with, and openness to the world, life and one's fellow-man' (Antoch 1981, 42). This is the aim of all human development. A 'sense of community' is not the antithesis of self-realisation. It is not disinterested self-denial, but committed dedication which serves one's fellow men (Seidenfuss 1981). Individual Psychology regards individuality and sociability, self-realisation and openness to the community, and self-assertion and self-dedication as being dialectically linked. In doing so it comes close to the concept of identity of social psychology.

Contrary to genetic theories which seek to explain human behaviour in terms of man's biological history, and *milieu* theories which attempt to explain it in terms of man's social environment, Individual Psychology believes that the subject is able actively to cope with his biological and social circumstances. The circumstances form both the raw material which the subject can mould at will, and that which imposes restrictions on him. This is called soft 'determinism' (Titze 1979). Theoretically then, Individual Psychology could also work on the subject's responsibility for his own life story. Besides, activity does not take place in objectively given conditions, but in a subjectively interpreted environment. A child's first experiences of life form his 'primary opinions' (Titze 1979) about himself, others, the world and life. These influence his perception (tendentious apperception), determine his lifestyle and how he will experience and master various life situations. As children's primary opinions are formed in the pre-speech period, these generally remain unconscious. Man's activities take place in a subjectively formed world and follow his unconscious private logic. This may seem strange to outsiders, but it is only really to be understood through the realisation that it is subjective. Anyone wishing to understand someone else and help him through therapy must seriously identify with the other person's situation to a sufficient degree (empathy) and credit the subjective reason of his (healthy or neurotic) life story.

The subject is also given credit for acting in respect of his feelings. These feelings are expressed in order to alleviate an irritating situation (Schmid 1977, Titze 1979, 208ff.). Guilt feelings, for example, relieve the burden of guilt, 'I am guilty, but at least I am sad about it (possibly different from others) and am spared any further consequences (to make good, for instance)'.

The individual gives his life a shape and meaning (aim in life) through his actions, and he lives his life with this aim in mind. What this implies is that man is pulled by final motives and not pushed by causal ones (Titze 1979). Drives also become effective, not as 'effectual causes' however, but as the starting-points of decisions (Müller 1954, 52). The final motive determines which decision will in fact be made. No human action or attitude, whether an expression of a happy life or a sympton of a neurotic disorder exists without a goal: it derives its meaning from its role as a *telos*.

However different the details of people's goals are, some similarity of structure does exist. Everyone inclines towards self-assurance (Kausen 1977c, 898ff.). In a threatening situation where they are found to be lacking, they attempt to find security for themselves either by really overcoming this defect or by becoming neurotic about it. For the most part, this is due to a lack of self-esteem (inferiority complex) which they endeavour to overcome through the experience of recognition (person-worth) from others. However, the lack of nourishment, affection and libidinal satisfaction can itself be experienced as a threat to their existence. The social self's tendency to seek security ('primacy of self-preservation over sexuality', Kausen 1977c, 894) is seen by Individual Psychology to represent the psyche's dynamic force. It results from a (ethologically ineradicable) primeval fear (*Ur-Angst*) of being expelled from the herd and no longer being able to live (fear of 'disgregation', Bilz 1956). If the individual has enough of a sense of community, then he does not attempt to find this security at others' expense, but by combining with others for the common good) compensating for an inferiority complex by increasing his self-esteem, which emerges from respect for, and recognition of other people). He will turn his complete attention to the community and forget his intention of seeking self-assurance, because this happens automatically. If the individual's sense of community is damaged, then he will resort to active-aggressive or passive-regressive methods to protect himself by dominating (compensating for shortcomings by neurotically striving for power). Therefore Individual Psychology views striving for power as a mistaken attempt (often unconscious) to compensate for the individual's real (although not necessarily so) experience of impotence. Striving for power can lead to openly destructive behaviour. However, it can also remain hidden: ostensible impotence (childlike behaviour, subordination, illness, submissiveness and suicide) then becomes an effective instrument in the secret exercise of power. Individual Psychology has described this (always reciprocal) neurotic behaviour in detail, which has a bearing not only on its relevance to socio-psychology, but also to its criticism of institutions (Sperber 1975).

The remainder of this article concerns Individual Psychology's challenge to religious belief and the Church. I must restrict myself to a small part of it. Adler was the first depth psychologist who through his work *Religion and Individual Psychology* (compare 1933b and 1933a) introduced a view of religion into depth psychology which was both comprehensible and worthy of respect. Adler allowed the 'concept of God' (*Gottesidee*) to have a place in his theory. Adler differed from Freud in regarding 'God' not as a projected illusion, but as a possible compensation. He agreed with Freud that 'God' was created by man (compare Metzger 1979 with Küng 1978), but maintained against him that 'God' ('the most brilliant manifestation of man's aim for perfection', Adler 1933b, 69) plays a positive role in providing security. As far as I can see this idea has scarcely had any effect on the theory of Individual Psychology after Adler (except Ringel 1973, 1975, 1978b, 1981, and Duhrssen 1960). The religious aspect of the patient is, however, now taken into account in the practice of Individual Psychology. Ringel: 'Anyone listening to the speech of the unconscious without prejudice . . . anyone whose thought processes are not blocked by ideological (*weltanschauliche*) bias will have to acknowledge the presence of God in the unconscious. . . . All this also means that within the framework of making the unconscious conscious the religious question will sooner or later become urgent in all depth psychology' (1981, 38). This remark is worthy of note, although it is questionable whether we can talk of God in the theological sense of the word, and whether we can generalise about mankind using neurotics as our point of departure (Ringel 1978, 181f.). The question which Ringel adds is more important: 'Why is there such a strong religious element in the unconscious, and why such a disquietingly weak one in the conscious? (Ringel 1981, 38). Yes, why? Are people incapable of coping with the religious aspect? Do they find no opportunity of communicating their questions and doubts within the Church? Are they alienated from their religious experience and conflict by Church defence mechanisms (taboo on problems and prevention of dialogue)?

Churchmen, theologians and those involved in religious education can learn about the use of religion by studying the motives and categories provided by Individual Psychology. Those who have subjective religion use it. However inadequately the theological aspect of (Christian) religion may be understood, we can scarcely disregard its anthropological function. Does religion represent revelation or compensation?—the alternative is a wrong one (Werbick 1981). Only a religion which is integrated into the psyche is one which is pro-man and likely to promote life. The content and lifestyles pertaining to the Christian faith are radical in so far as they reflect and formulate the protection of human life. Therefore human life should not be reduced to mental life. The whole man comprising his biological, economic, environmental, emotional and social needs wants to live.

Detailed research carried out by Individual Psychology has revealed that (exaggerated) humility and altruism on the part of Christians are compensations for neurotic feelings of inferiority, although, at the same time, they both dominate and are credited with having a high Christian ethical code. Individual Psychology suspects the existence of desperate attempts by the deeply insecure psyche to find security in the doctrine of infallibility. The Church does not restrict itself to maintaining that truth illuminates revelation, it goes on to maintain (metalinguistically) that the certainty of this truth is beyond doubt. This it does by referring to the infallibility of those who spread this truth. Is that security for those who hear the truth, or personal security for those who propound it? The danger involved in a reciprocal relationship between theology and Individual Psychology is seen by the very fact that it is possible to say and ask such things. Within the Church, many relationships are in an unhealthy state because of the exercise of power. The talk of radical brotherly love cannot disguise this state of affairs. The Church is seen to symbolise dominance rather than to be orientated towards man; insistence on legalism rather than trusting everyone to be responsible enough to make independent judgments; forced subordination instead of encouragement to feel free and engage in free relations. This all betrays powerlessness, mistrust and anxiety (*Angst*). It cannot be understood without realising that those who behave in such a manner feel inferior. At present sexuality is discussed more openly in the Church, but the problems of wielding power and the subordination to power, as self-protecting mechanisms within the Church, still remain repressed.

Lastly, non-believers are often said to have been led astray, to be stupid, complacent . . .; we read such things in official Church texts. Individual Psychology teaches that man must be understood against the background of his personal logic. The stranger is not understood until he is seen as a subjectively rational being. If the Church is to take appropriate action in the secular world, it must recognise this fact.

Translated by Pauline A. Stuart

Bibliography

Adler, A. (1933a) *Der Sinn des Lebens* (Frankfurt 1973).

Adler, A. (1933b) *Religion und Individualpsychologie* (Frankfurt 1975).

Antoch, R. F. (1979) 'Zum Verhaltnis zwischen der Individualpsychologie und der Verhaltenstherapie' in *Zeitschrift für Individualpsychologie (ZIP)* 4 (1979) 104-120.

Antoch, R. F. (1980a) 'Das Unbewusste und die Einheit des Lebensstils bei Adler' in *ZIP* 5 (1980) 9-131.

Antoch, R. F. (1980b) 'Besprechung von Titze' (1979) in *ZIP* 5 (1980) 117-119.

Antoch, R. F. (1981) 'Anmerkungen zum Thema "Gemeinschafsgefuhl"' *ZIP* 6 (1981) 40-42.

Bilz, R. (1956) 'Die Kuckucksterz' in *Viktor von Weizsacker. Arzt im Wirrsal der Zeit* ed. R. Vogel (Gottingen 1956) 99-119.

Birnbaum, F. (1948) 'Gibt es eine Konvergenz der tiefenpsychologischen Lehrmeinungen?' in *Internationale Zeitschrift für Individualpsychologie* 17 (1948) 156-171.

Duhrssen, A. (1960) *Psychotherapie bei Kindern und Jugendlichen* (Gottingen 4/ 1971).

Kausen, R. (1977a) 'Die Wirkungen der Individualpsychologie heute' in *Die Psychologie des 20. Jahrhunderts* (Zürich 1977) III pp. 643-656.

Kausen, R. (1977b) 'Warum Wechselheit von Anfang an?' in *Situationsbewaltigung durch Fragen* ed. Ringel and Brandl (Wien-Freiburg-Basel 1977) 25-40.

Kausen, R. (1977c) 'Zur Theorie der Individualpsychologie' in *Handbuch der Psychologie* (Gottingen 1977) VIII/1 pp. 889-919.

Küng, H. (1978) *Existiert Gott?* (München-Zürich 1978).

Metzger, W. (1979) 'Alfred Adler und die Religion' in *Die Psychologie des 20. Jahrhunderts* (Zürich 1979) XV pp. 239-244.

Müller, A. (1954) *Du sollst ein Segen sein* (Schwarzenberg 1954).

Ringel, E. (1973) 'Selbstschädigung durch Neurose' (Wien-Freiburg-Basel 1975).

Ringel, E. (1975) 'Religion und Neurose' in *Religion und Tiefenpsychologie* ed. G. Rombold (Linz 1975) 83-100.

Ringel, E. (1978a) 'Zur Identitätsfindung der Individualpsychologie' in *Beitrage zur Individualpsychologie* ed. Kausen and Mohr (München 1978) 145-154.

Ringel, E. (1978b) 'Religion und Neurose' in *Herderkorrespondenz* 32 (1978) 174-182.

Ringel, E. (1981) 'Begegnung zwischen Tiefenpsychologie und Glaube' in *Pastoralblatt* 33 (1981) 37-49.

Schmid, R. (1977) 'Finalität der Angst' in *ZIP* 2 (1977) 48-57.

Seidenfuss, J. (1981) 'Die Entwicklung von Gemeinschaftsgefuhl als Selbstverwirklichung, Anpassung und sociale Evolution' in *ZIP* 6 (1981) 57-70.

Sperber, M. (1975) *Zur Analyse der Tyrannis* (Wien 1975).

Sperber, M. (1978) *Individuum und Gemeinschaft* (Stuttgart 1978).

Spiel, O. (1948) 'Gemeinschaft als Ideal und Realität' in *Internationale Zeitschrift für Individualpsychologie* 17 (1948) 145-156.

Spiel, W. (1978) 'Individualpsychologie und Verhaltenstherapie' in *Beiträge zur Individualpsychologie* ed. Kausen and Mohr (München 1978) 208-214.

Titze, M. (1979) *Lebensziel und Lebensstil* (München 1979).

Werbick, J. (1981) 'Und der Mensch schuf Gott nach seinem Bild' in *Zeitschrift für die Praxis des Religionsunterrichts* 11 (1981) 156-160.

Marie McCarthy

Family Therapy: New Paradigm, New Challenge

1. THE EMERGENCE OF FAMILY THERAPY

ONE OF the more significant developments among the therapeutic disciplines has been the emergence, over the past twenty years, of the field of family therapy. The field has grown rapidly, with practice outdistancing the development of theory. This gap which has existed between theory and practice is testimony both to the pragmatic bent of the discipline and to the sense of urgency felt by therapists seeking to assist troubled families. In recent years, as the field of family therapy has become more firmly established and has developed into somewhat distinct approaches, efforts have been made to systematise the field and to articulate a theoretical framework which is genuinely informed by and informing of practice.[1] Such efforts face an immediate, underlying difficulty central to a consideration of the nature and implications of the field of family therapy. This is the problem of definition. The nature and structure of the family are not easily definable, for the family is intricately interwoven with and reflective of the society in which it exists. There is not one form of family and family structure. There are many forms and structures of families, each incorporating a unique set of cultural values, each shifting, developing, changing both in response to and as a challenge to the society in which it exists. Consequently no single definition of the family will be entirely adequate.

The field of family therapy has, to some extent, addressed this problem by moving away from definitions of the family which focus on function, role, structure, or size, and moving toward definitions which offer a dynamic formulation of the interpersonal, emotional processes which constitute the experience of family.[2] The family, as viewed from the perspective of family therapy, is a psychological unit with system properties. It is a dynamic unit characterised by interlocking, interpersonal relationships which demand emotional investment and provide emotional nurturance. Additionally, it is a major means of social control and a highly structured social system with appropriate task and role divisions.[3]

2. A NEW PARADIGM

The field of family therapy incorporates within it a reconceptualisation of the nature of the family and of the nature and cause of psychopathology. Family therapy is generally defined in contrast to individually oriented therapies which view the individual as the locus of pathology and the essential unit of change. An individual orientation tends to see family relationships as a complicating factor within the life of the individual. Therapeutic intervention is aimed at changing the individual, thus allowing for subsequent changes within the family system. A family oriented therapeutic approach, contrastingly, sees the total family as a system of interlocking relationships. Intervention is aimed at the level of the family system and is based on the assumption that changes in family relationships will lead to changes in each person. The family and family interrelations constitute the essential unit of change. Pathology is viewed as a response to certain interactional patterns within the family system.

The reconceptualisation of the nature of the family and of the nature and cause of psychopathology which has evolved out of the practice of family therapy has introduced a major paradigm shift on at least two levels.[4] On one level the field of family therapy has moved away from a linear model of causality to a circular, evolutionary paradigm, incorporating the principles of spontaneous variation and natural selection, viewing the family as capable, therefore, of sudden transformations. In this model, equilibrium and disequilibrium, stasis and change, involve the entire complex of family relations and dynamics in a process of reciprocal relations of causality. On another level, the epistemological shift from a linear to a circular model of causality has been accompanied by a reconceptualisation of the self as fundamentally social, rather than fundamentally individual, in nature. Family therapy, then, is a unique blend of psychological and systems theory, therapeutic technique, cultural values, and ethical and religio-ethical norms. And it may be, as Joan Stein suggests that the normative positions and value judgments concerning health and illness, which are often implicit within the various schools of family therapy, are among the primary shapers of theory and practice.[5]

3. VARYING APPROACHES TO FAMILY TREATMENT

The field of family therapy does not divide neatly into distinct 'schools' with clearly distinguishable sets of theories, goals, and techniques. There are more commonalities than differences among the various approaches to family therapy, and the differences which do exist, while important, are matters of degree and emphasis rather than of stark dichotomies. All the varying approaches to family treatment are rooted in a systems conceptualisation of the family, focusing on changing family interactional patterns. The differences which do exist in approach and style may be as much in response to the differing structures, capabilities, and developmental levels of families being seen, as they are in response to differing theoretical frameworks.

Among the various schema suggested for distinguishing systems of family therapy,[6] a particularly useful framework is to view approaches to family therapy as existing on a continuum stretching from an individual, intrapsychic orientation to a systems orientation. The major figures in the field of family therapy generally can be seen as operating out of one of three models: a psychoanalytic model, a communicative-interactive model, or an integrative model. The *psychoanalytic model* focuses on individual, intrapsychic forces, giving secondary status to dimensions of family interaction. Emphasis is placed on the individual patient as the container of pathology with the rest of the family being viewed as a stress factor. Relationships and environmental forces are viewed as separate from and external to the patient's intrapsychic life. Major figures employing a psychoanalytic model of family therapy include Nathan Ackerman, James Framo, Charles Kramer, and Lyman Wynne. The *communicative-interactive approach* represents the opposite end of the spectrum from a psychoanalytically oriented approach. It is characterised by an almost exclusive focus on the family system, viewing symptoms as a result of family interactions. Pathology is understood to be the result of dysfunctional communication patterns within the family system. The goal of this approach is to enable clearer communication at both the verbal and the non-verbal level. The major theorists and practitioners of the communicative-interactive approach include Gregory Bateson, Jay Haley, Don Jackson, Mara Selvini Palozzoli and the Milan Associates, and Virginia Satir. The *integrative model* of family therapy incorporates insights from both the psychoanalytic and the communicative-interactive approaches. It recognises the importance of intrapsychic and interpersonal dynamics and of environmental factors which can impinge on the family system. All these dimensions are seen as interacting with each other to produce the person in the present situation. The integrative approach focuses on the structure of the family, the various roles of family members, and the establishment and maintenance of appropriate role and generation boundaries. Murray Bowen and Salvador Minuchin are among those who employ an integrative approach to family therapy.

It is possible to view these various approaches to family therapy as incorporating to differing degrees the central elements of the paradigm shift which has been pointed to. The psychoanalytic approach, while recognising the importance of the family, does not fully integrate the epistemological implications which the shift to a systems approach entails. It continues to employ a linear causal model and to overemphasise the individual, autonomous dimensions of the self. On the other hand, the communicative-interactive approach, in its attempt to be faithful to a systems orientation, tends to discard all elements of a psychoanalytic approach. In doing so, it disregards the psychoanalytic roots of the entire family therapy movement and also fails to incorporate a genuinely circular model of causality by ignoring the interaction of both intrapsychic and interpersonal dynamics in the formation of the social self. The integrative model most fully recognises the validity of the new paradigm, incorporating the central features of both a psychoanalytic and a systems orientation into a new model which emphasises the importance of interactions among individual, familial, and environmental factors, thus opening up new directions for growth and transformation.

Despite the differences in theoretical framework and emphases which have been cited, certain common goals and themes emerge from an examination of the various systems of family therapy. Some of the most frequently mentioned goals of family therapy include improved communication, increased autonomy and individuation, increased empathy, more flexible leadership and improved role correspondence.[7] In addition, a cluster of concepts emerges from the different approaches to family therapy, pointing to a significant theme underlying all forms of family therapy. These concepts include such notions as differentiation, enmeshment, pseudo-mutuality, autonomy, individuation, emotional divorce, and the undifferentiated family ego mass. Each of these concepts embodies an underlying assumption concerning the appropriate, healthy, or normative model for family interrelationships. Each proposes what might be called a model of mutuality; that is, a model for the appropriate balance of give and take between the individual and the family in relation to such issues as autonomy and dependence, the rigidity and flexibility of system boundaries, and the closeness or distance of affectional ties. Each of these concepts is, at the same time, a major shaper of theoretical constructs and therapeutic interventions.

4. MUTUALITY: A CONTACT POINT BETWEEN FAMILY THERAPY AND THEOLOGY

These models of mutuality which inform the various systems of family therapy are not strictly scientific in character. They are rather, ethical and religio-ethical models of human relationship. As such, they confront theology and faith with the need for a new understanding of the nature and meaning of self-actualisation and self-sacrifice. They challenge theology to adopt a more social understanding of the nature of the self and to articulate a model of mutuality which incorporates dimensions of self-actualisation and self-sacrifice into a new and viable model of self-transcendence and transformation.[8]

The core of the mutual challenge between systems of family therapy and theology can be focused in terms of a question: what model of mutuality is employed in choosing between the conflicting needs, wants, and desires of the individual and of the family—a model of self-actualisation giving priority to the individual; a model of self-sacrifice giving priority to the family system; or a model of self-transcendence and transformation which incorporates both dimensions into a genuinely new possibility? Systems of family therapy, to the extent that they incorporate an evolutionary paradigm based on a social definition of the self and a model of reciprocal relations of causality do point to the possibility of sudden transformations within family systems. The challenge to theology and the faith is to incorporate the epistemological shift pointed to by the therapies into a new understanding of and a new language for self-fulfilment. A self-actualisation model based on the assumption of an identity between Christianity and culture or a self-sacrificial model based on the assumption of a contradiction between Christianity and culture are equally inadequate. Both are rooted in the old paradigm of the self as fundamentally individual. Once a social definition of the self is adopted, the meaning of the terms self-actualisation and self-sacrifice changes. Both become means to an end—the end of a genuine self-fulfilment which is realised through self-transcendence and transformation. Both then operate in the service of a mutuality which offers a new, graced possibility for being-with-others-in-the-world.

Notes

1. See especially L. Hoffman *Foundations of Family Therapy* (New York 1981); C. Kramer *Becoming a Family Therapist* (New York 1980).
2. Even here it is important to recognise the family therapy movement as a largely western phenomenon. The understanding of family and the values which that understanding incorporates will unavoidably reflect a western world view.
3. See Kramer, in the work cited in note 1, pp. 10-44. J. Stein *The Family As A Unit of Study and Treatment* (region IX Rehabilitation Research Institute, Monograph One) University of Washington, 1969.
4. See Group for the Advancement of Psychiatry *The Field of Family Therapy—Report #78* (New York 1970) chaps. 4 and 6; Hoffman, in the work cited in note 1, chap. 1; Kramer, in the work cited in note 1, Introduction.
5. Stein, in the work cited in note 3, p. 3.
6. See for example GAP report #78, cited in note 4, chap. 6; Kramer, in the work cited in note 1, chap. 5; Stein, in the work cited in note 3.
7. See GAP report #78, cited in note 4, p. 553.
8. See D. Tracy 'The Catholic Model of Caritas: Self-Transcendence and Transformation' in *The Family In Crisis or In Transition*, *Concilium* 121 (New York 1979).

Contributors

WOLFGANG BARTHOLOMÄUS was born in Osnabrück, Germany, in 1934. He studied philosophy and theology in Frankfurt am Main, religious education, education and the science of communication in Munich, and depth psychology in Vienna. He gained his doctorate in theology in 1972 and is now professor for religious education and kerygmatics in the Catholic theological faculty of the University of Tübingen. His publications include *Evangelium als Information. Elemente einer theologischen kommunikationstheorie* (Zürich 1972); *Kleine Predigtlehre* (Zürich 1974); in collaboration with A. Stock *Wissenschaftstheorie und Studienreform* (Zürich 1975); *Christsein lernen* (Zürich 1981).

DON BROWNING, professor of religion and psychological studies at the University of Chicago since 1977, was born in 1934 and ordained in 1952 as minister of the Christian Church (Disciples of Christ). He studied theology and psychology and received in 1964 his doctorate at the Divinity School of the University of Chicago. He has published many articles on psychology and pastoral care and the following works: *Atonement and Psychotherapy* (Philadelphia 1966); *Generative Man: Society and Good Man in Philip Rieff, Norman Brown, Erich Fromm, and Erik Erikson* (Philadelphia 1973); *The Moral Context of Care* (Philadelphia 1976); *Pluralism and Personality* (Lewisburg 1980).

LEE CORMIE was born in 1943 in Troy, New York. He received a PhD from The Divinity School, University of Chicago, and is currently teaching in the areas of theology and the social sciences, social ethics with special interest in the economy, work and the family, and liberation theologies on the Faculty of Theology, St Michael's College and the Toronto School of Theology, Toronto. He is also executive secretary of the Theologians Project of Theology in the Americas; this is a five-year ecumenical project bringing together social activists, church leaders, theologians, and social scientists with the aim of contributing to the revitalisation of theology and theological education through commitment to justice and liberation for the oppressed.

JACK DOMINIAN was born in Athens in 1929. He was educated in Greece, India and England, qualified at Cambridge, England, as doctor in 1955 and as psychiatrist in 1961. He is now senior consultant psychiatrist, Central Middlesex Hospital, London. His publications include: *Psychiatry and the Christian* (London 1961) *Marital Breakdown* (London 1967); *Christian Marriage* (London 1968); *The Church and Sexual Revolution* (London 1971); *Cycles of Affirmation* (London 1975); *Depression* (London 1976); *From Cosmos to Love* (London 1976); *Proposals for a New Sexual Ethic* (London 1977); *Marriage, Faith and Love* (London 1981).

JARL E. DYRUD, MD, is a psychiatrist and psychoanalyst, professor of psychiatry in the division of biological sciences and a member of the associated faculty of the Divinity School at the University of Chicago. He was born in Maddock, North Dakota in 1921, and received his MD degree from the Johns Hopkins University in 1945. Trained in psychiatry, psychoanalysis and behaviour research, he has published in all three areas of interest. Before going to the University of Chicago in 1968 he was director of research at Chestnut Lodge Hospital, Rochville, Maryland. He taught at Howard University and was a lecturer in pastoral theology at the Jesuit Theologate, Woodstock, Maryland. He has written many articles in the fields of his principal interests.

DONALD EVANS, born in 1927, is professor of philosophy at the University of Toronto, and a minister of The United Church of Canada. His works include *The Logic of Self-Involvement; Communist Faith and Christian Faith; Faith; Authenticity and Morality* and *Struggle and Fulfillment*, which brings together therapeutic and religious experience, especially in the struggle between basic truat and basic distrust. Since 1969 he has been involved in Therafields, a Toronto therapeutic community. For several years he has also been learning methods of meditation from a variety of Christian and non-Christian teachers.

JAMES W. FOWLER serves as professor of theology and human development and director of the Center for Faith Development at Candler School of Theology of Emory University. Professor Fowler, a United Methodist minister, received his doctorate in religion and society from Harvard University in 1971. His books include *To See the Kingdom: The Theological Vision of H. Richard Niebuhr* (1974) and *Stages of Faith* (1981). He is co-author or editor of *Life-Maps: Conversations on the Journey of Faith* (1978); *Trajectories in Faith* (1980); and *Toward Moral and Religious Maturity* (1980).

JUDITH VAN HERIK is assistant professor of religious studies at the Pennsylvania State University, University Park, PA. Her doctorate is from the University of Chicago Divinity School in the area of religion and psychological studies. She is author of *Freud on Femininity and Faith* (Berkeley, Los Angeles and London 1981), which analyses relationships between Freud's theories of gender difference and of religion.

STEVEN KEPNES teaches psychology of religion and modern Jewish and Christian thought at Middlebury College in Middlebury, Vermont. He worked for two years as a pastoral psychotherapist at the Community Pastoral Counseling and Consultation Center affiliated with Lutheran General Hospital in Park Ridge, Illinois. His University of Chicago dissertation is titled 'Martin Buber's Stories and Contemporary Narrative Theory'. He has written review articles for the *Journal of Religion* and *Religious Studies Review*.

WALTER LOWE, professor of systematic theology, was born in Madison, Wisconsin, in 1940. He studied theology and philosophy and received in 1972 his doctorate in religious studies at Yale University. He has published articles on Christology, psychoanalysis and the problem of evil; and the following works: *Mystery and the Unconscious: A Study in the Thought of Paul Ricoeur* (Metuchen NJ 1977) and *Evil and the Unconscious* (to be published by Scholars Press, Chico CA).

BRIAN MAHAN was born in Cambridge, Massachusetts, in 1948. Currently a PhD candidate at the Divinity School of the University of Chicago, he also holds graduate degrees from Boston College and Harvard Divinity School. He is co-editor (with L. Dale Richesin) of *The Challenge of Liberation Theology: A First World Response* (Maryknoll, NY 1981) and is one of several contributors to *Trajectories in Faith*, James W. Fowler, Robin W. Lovin, *et al.* (Nashville 1980). The subject of his thesis project is the religious thought of William James.

E. DOYLE McCARTHY, PhD, assistant professor of sociology at Fordham University, was born in 1944. She is author of various articles in the fields of social psychiatry and social theory.

MARIE McCARTHY was born in Chicago, Illinois, in 1942. She holds an MA in theology from the Catholic Theological Union in Chicago, Illinois, and the MA in religion and psychological studies from the University of Chicago. She has taught pastoral counselling at the Catholic Theological Union in Chicago and has given workshops in various cities in the United States. She is currently a PhD candidate in religion and psychological studies at the University of Chicago.

SEBASTIAN MOORE was born in Madras, India, in 1917. Educated in England, by the Benedictines and others between 1924-34, he served in the Royal Navy between 1934-38. He entered the novitiate at Downside (Benedictine) in 1938. He majored in English literature at Cambridge, under F. R. Leavis, with honours in 1945. He studied theology at Sant Anselmo, Rome, 1946-51, obtaining a doctorate for work on Irenaeus. He was editor of *The Downside Review* between 1954-60, and taught theology and English at Downside between 1951-60. He did special studies with Bernard Lonergan in Rome in 1960. He served on a parish in Liverpool between 1960-70, during which time the following works were published: *God is a New Language, No Exit, The Dreamer not the Dream, Beyond the Deluge*, and *The Experience of Prayer*. Since 1971, he has been campus minister and professor of theology at Marquette University, Milwaukee, during which time the following works were published: *The Crucified is No Stranger, The Fire and the Rose are One*. In publication now: *The Inner Loneliness*. His main concern throughout has been the psychological and, more generally, modern-cultural, appropriation of the mystery of Jesus Christ.

CARL D. SCHNEIDER is currently a senior staff counsellor at the Pastoral Psychotherapy Institute of Parkside Human Services Corporation, Lutheran General Medical Center, Park Ridge, Illinois. Dr Schneider holds a MDiv degree, *magna cum laude*, from Union Theological Seminary in New York City and a PhD from Harvard University in psychology and religion. The author of several articles and a book *Shame, Exposure and Privacy*, Dr Schneider has taught, among other places, at Antioch Graduate School, the Chicago Cluster of Theological Schools, DePaul University, Harvard University, Indiana University, Meadville/Lombard Theological School, Northeastern Illinois University, Schiller College, and the University of Chicago. A United Methodist clergy person, Dr Schneider is a member of the American Association for Marriage and Family Therapy, the American Association of Pastoral Counselors, the Family Mediation Association, the American Orthopsychiatric Association, and a registered psychologist in the State of Illinois. As a pastoral psychotherapist, Dr Schneider provides therapy for individuals, couples, families and groups.

RUDOLF SIEBERT was born in Frankfurt am Main in 1927. He studied theology, philosophy, philology and history at the Universities of Mainz and Münster, and at the Catholic University of America, Washington DC. He has widely taught and lectured in Europe, the USA and Canada. From 1962-65 he taught sociology, economics and theology at St Agnes and Loyola College in Baltimore, Maryland. Since 1975, Professor Siebert has been professor of religion and society in the Religion Department of Western Michigan University, Kalamazoo, Michigan. In the last three decades, he has concentrated his teaching, lecturing and writing in Europe and North America on the philosophy of G. W. F. Hegel, the Frankfurt School of philosophy and sociology, and critical political theology. In 1977 he initiated and has since directed the international course on *The Future of Religion* in the Inter-University Centre of Post Graduate Studies in Dubrovnik, Yugoslavia. He is founder of *The Centre for Humanistic Future Studies* at Western Michigan University. His main works are: *From Critical Theory of*

Society to Theology of Communicative Praxis; *Hegel's Philosophy of History: Theological, Humanistic, Scientific Elements*; *Hegel's Concept of Marriage* and *Family: Subjective Freedom*; *Horkheimer's Critical Sociology of Religion: The Relative and the Transcendent*; *Reason, Freedom and Change: A Christian Encounter with Hegel* (all by Washington DC University Press of America, 1979-1982). Rudolf and Margaret (+ 20 October 1978) Siebert are the parents of seven children.

CONCILIUM

1. (Vol. 1 No. 1) **Dogma.** Ed. Edward Schillebeeckx. 86pp.
2. (Vol. 2 No. 1) **Liturgy.** Ed. Johannes Wagner. 100pp.
3. (Vol. 3 No. 1) **Pastoral.** Ed. Karl Rahner. 104pp.
4. (Vol. 4 No. 1) **Ecumenism.** Hans Küng. 108pp.
5. (Vol. 5 No. 1) **Moral Theology.** Ed. Franz Bockle 98pp.
6. (Vol. 6 No. 1) **Church and World.** Ed. Johannes Baptist Metz. 92pp.
7. (Vol. 7 No. 1) **Church History.** Roger Aubert. 92pp.
8. (Vol. 8 No. 1) **Canon Law.** Ed. Teodoro Jimenez Urresti and Neophytos Edelby. 96pp.
9. (Vol. 9 No. 1) **Spirituality.** Ed. Christian Duquoc. 88pp.
10. (Vol. 10 No. 1) **Scripture.** Ed. Pierre Benoit and Roland Murphy. 92pp.
11. (Vol. 1 No. 2) **Dogma.** Ed. Edward Schillebeeckx. 88pp.
12. (Vol. 2 No. 2) **Liturgy.** Ed. Johannes Wagner. 88pp.
13. (Vol. 3 No. 2) **Pastoral.** Ed. Karl Rahner. 84pp.
14. (Vol. 4 No. 2) **Ecumenism.** Ed. Hans Küng. 96pp.
15. (Vol. 5 No. 2) **Moral Theology.** Ed. Franz Bockle. 88pp.
16. (Vol. 6 No. 2) **Church and World.** Ed. Johannes Baptist Metz. 84.pp.
17. (Vol. 7 No. 2) **Church History.** Ed. Roger Aubert. 96pp.
18. (Vol. 8 No. 2) **Religious Freedom.** Ed. Neophytos Edelby and Teodoro Jimenez Urresti. 96pp.
19. (Vol. 9 No. 2) **Religionless Christianity?** Ed. Christian Duquoc. 96pp.
20. (Vol. 10 No. 2) **The Bible and Tradition.** Ed. Pierre Benoit and Roland E. Murphy. 96pp.
21. (Vol. 1 No 3) **Revelation and Dogma.** Ed. Edward Schillebeeckx. 88pp.
22. (Vol. 2 No. 3) **Adult Baptism and Initiation.** Ed. Johannes Wagner. 96pp.
23. (Vol. 3 No. 3) **Atheism and Indifference.** Ed. Karl Rahner. 92pp.
24. (Vol. 4 No. 3) **The Debate on the Sacraments.** Ed. Hans Küng. 92pp.
25. (Vol. 5 No. 3) **Morality, Progress and History.** Ed. Franz Bockle. 84pp.
26. (Vol. 6 No. 3) **Evolution.** Ed. Johannes Baptist Metz. 88pp.
27. (Vol. 7 No. 3) **Church History.** Ed. Roger Aubert. 92pp.
28. (Vol. 8 No. 3) **Canon Law—Theology and Renewal.** Ed. Neophytos Edelby and Teodoro Jimenez Urresti. 92pp.
29. (Vol. 9 No. 3) **Spirituality and Politics.** Ed. Christian Duquoc. 84pp.
30. (Vol. 10 No. 3) **The Value of the Old Testament.** Ed. Pierre Benoit and Roland Murphy. 92pp.
31. (Vol. 1 No. 4) **Man, World and Sacrament.** Ed. Edward Schillebeeckx. 84pp.
32. (Vol. 2 No. 4) **Death and Burial: Theology and Liturgy.** Ed. Johannes Wagner. 88pp.
33. (Vol. 3 No. 4) **Preaching the Word of God.** Ed. Karl Rahner. 96pp.
34. (Vol. 4 No. 4) **Apostolic by Succession?** Ed. Hans Küng. 96pp.
35. (Vol. 5 No. 4) **The Church and Social Morality.** Ed. Franz Bockle. 92pp.
36. (Vol. 6 No. 4) **Faith and the World of Politics.** Ed. Johannes Baptist Metz 96pp.
37. (Vol. 7 No. 4) **Prophecy.** Ed. Roger Aubert. 80pp.
38. (Vol. 8 No. 4) **Order and the Sacraments.** Ed. Neophytos Edelby and Teodoro Jimenez Urresti. 96pp.
39. (Vol. 9 No. 4) **Christian Life and Eschatology.** Ed. Christian Duquoc. 94pp.
40. (Vol. 10 No. 4) **The Eucharist: Celebrating the Presence of the Lord.** Ed. Pierre Benoit and Roland Murphy. 88pp.
41. (Vol. 1 No. 5) **Dogma.** Ed. Edward Schillebeeckx. 84pp.
42. (Vol. 2 No. 5) **The Future of the Liturgy.** Ed. Johannes Wagner. 92pp.
43. (Vol. 3 No. 5) **The Ministry and Life of Priests Today.** Ed. Karl Rahner. 104pp.
44. (Vol. 4 No. 5) **Courage Needed.** Ed. Hans Küng. 92pp.
45. (Vol. 5 No. 5) **Profession and Responsibility in Society.** Ed. Franz Bockle. 84pp.
46. (Vol. 6 No. 5) **Fundamental Theology.** Ed. Johannes Baptist Metz. 84pp.
47. (Vol. 7 No. 5) **Sacralization in the History of the Church.** Ed. Roger Aubert. 80pp.
48. (Vol. 8 No. 5) **The Dynamism of Canon Law.** Ed. Neophytos Edelby and Teodoro Jimenez Urresti. 92pp.
49. (Vol. 9 No. 5) **An Anxious Society Looks to the Gospel.** Ed. Christian Duquoc. 80pp.
50. (Vol. 10 No. 5) **The Presence and Absence of God.** Ed. Pierre Benoit and Roland Murphy. 88pp.
51. (Vol. 1 No. 6) **Tension between Church and Faith.** Ed. Edward Schillebeeckx. 160pp.
52. (Vol. 2 No. 6) **Prayer and Community.** Ed. Herman Schmidt. 156pp.
53. (Vol. 3 No. 6) **Catechetics for the Future.** Ed. Alois Müller. 168pp.
54. (Vol. 4 No. 6) **Post-Ecumenical Christianity.** Ed. Hans Küng. 168pp.
55. (Vol. 5 No. 6) **The Future of Marriage as Institution.** Ed. Franz Bockle. 180pp.
56. (Vol. 6 No. 6) **Moral Evil Under Challenge.** Ed. Johannes Baptist Metz. 160pp.
57. (Vol. 7 No. 6) **Church History at a Turning Point.** Ed. Roger Aubert. 160pp.
58. (Vol. 8 No. 6) **Structures of the Church's Presence in the World of Today.** Ed. Teodoro Jimenez Urresti. 160pp.
59. (Vol. 9 No. 6) **Hope.** Ed. Christian Duquoc. 160pp.
60. (Vol. 10 No. 6) **Immortality and Resurrection.** Ed. Pierre Benoit and Roland Murphy. 160
61. (Vol. 1 No. 7) **The Sacra Administration of Reconc** Ed. Edward Schillebeeck 160pp.
62. (Vol. 2 No. 7) **Worship Christian Man Today.** Ed Herman Schmidt. 156pp.
63. (Vol. 3 No. 7) **Democrat of the Church.** Ed. Alois Müller. 160pp.
64. (Vol. 4 No. 7) **The Petri Ministry in the Church.** Hans Küng. 160pp.
65. (Vol. 5 No. 7) **The Mani of Man.** Ed. Franz Bockl 144pp.
66. (Vol. 6 No. 7) **Fundamer Theology in the Church.** Johannes Baptist Metz. 1
67. (Vol. 7 No. 7) **The Self-Understanding of the Church.** Ed. Roger Aub 144pp.
68. (Vol. 8 No. 7) **Contestati the Church.** Ed. Teodoro Jimenez Urresti. 152pp.
69. (Vol. 9 No. 7) **Spiritualit Public or Private?** Ed. C Duquoc. 156pp.
70. (Vol. 10 No. 7) **Theology Exegesis and Proclamatio** Roland Murphy. 144pp.
71. (Vol. 1 No. 8) **The Bisho the Unity of the Church.** Edward Schillebeeckx. 1
72. (Vol. 2 No. 8) **Liturgy ar Ministry.** Ed. Herman Sc 160pp.
73. (Vol. 3 No. 8) **Reform of Church.** Ed. Alois Mülle Norbert Greinacher. 152
74. (Vol. 4 No. 8) **Mutual Recognition of Ecclesial Ministries?** Ed. Hans Kü Walter Kasper. 152pp.
75. (Vol. 5 No. 8) **Man in a Society.** Ed. Franz Bockl 160pp.
76. (Vol. 6 No. 8) **The God Question.** Ed. Johannes Metz. 156pp.
77. (Vol. 7 No. 8) **Election-Consensus-Reception.** Ed Giuseppe Alberigo and A Weiler. 156pp.
78. (Vol. 8 No. 8) **Celibacy c Catholic Priest.** Ed. Willi Bassett and Peter Huizin 160pp.
79. (Vol. 9 No. 8) **Prayer.** E Christian Duquoc and Cl Geffré. 126pp.
80. (Vol. 10 No. 8) **Ministrie Church.** Ed. Bas van Ier Roland Murphy. 152pp.
81. **The Persistence of Religio** Andrew Greeley and Gre Baum. 0 8164 2537 X 16
82. **Liturgical Experience of** Ed. Herman Schmidt anc Power. 0 8164 2538 8 14
83. **Truth and Certainty.** Ed. Edward Schillebeeckx an van Iersel. 0 8164 2539 6
84. **Political Commitment and Christian Community.** Ec Müller and Norbert Grei 0 8164 2540 X 156pp.
85. **The Crisis of Religious La** Ed. Johannes Baptist Me Jean-Pierre Jossua. 0 8164 2541 8 144pp.
86. **Humanism and Christiani**

audde Geffré. 0 8164 2542 6
4pp.
e Future of Christian
arriage. Ed. William Bassett
d Peter Huizing.
8164 2575 2.
larization in the Church. Ed.
ans Küng and Walter Kasper.
8164 2572 8 156pp.
iritual Revivals. Ed. Christian
uquoc and Casiano Floristán.
8164 2573 6 156pp.
wer and the Word of God.
l. Franz Bockle and Jacques
arie Pohier.
8164 2574 4 156pp.
he Church as Institution. Ed.
regory Baum and Andrew
reeley. 0 8164 2575 2 168pp.
litics and Liturgy. Ed.
erman Schmidt and David
ower. 0 8164 2576 0 156pp.
sus Christ and Human
eedom. Ed. Edward
hillebeeckx and Bas van
rsel. 0 8164 2577 9 168pp.
ne Experience of Dying. Ed.
orbert Greinacher and Alois
üller. 0 8164 2578 7 156pp.
heology of Joy. Ed. Johannes
aptist Metz and Jean-Pierre
ssua. 0 8164 2579 5 164pp.
he Mystical and Political
imension of the Christian
aith. Ed. Claude Geffré and
ustavo Guttierez.
8164 2580 9 168pp.
he Future of the Religious Life.
d. Peter Huizing and William
assett. 0 8164 2094 7 96pp.
hristians and Jews. Ed. Hans
üng and Walter Kasper.
8164 2095 5 96pp.
xperience of the Spirit. Ed.
eter Huizing and William
assett. 0 8164 2096 3 144pp.
exuality in Contemporary
atholicism. Ed. Franz Bockle
nd Jacques Marie Pohier.
8164 2097 1 126pp.
thnicity. Ed. Andrew Greeley
nd Gregory Baum.
8164 2145 5 120pp.
iturgy and Cultural Religious
raditions. Ed. Herman Schmidt
nd David Power. 0 8164 2146 2
20pp.
Personal God? Ed. Edward
chillebeeckx and Bas van
ersel. 0 8164 2149 8 142pp.
he Poor and the Church. Ed.
orbert Greinacher and Alois
lüller. 0 8164 2147 1 128pp.
hristianity and Socialism. Ed.
ohannes Baptist Metz and
ean-Pierre Jossua.
8164 2148 X 144pp.
he Churches of Africa: Future
rospects. Ed. Claude Geffré
nd Bertrand Luneau.
8164 2150 1 128pp.
udgement in the Church. Ed.
Villiam Bassett and Peter
luizing. 0 8164 2166 8 128pp.
Vhy Did God Make Me? Ed.
lans Küng and Jürgen
loltmann. 0 8164 2167 6 112pp.

109. **Charisms in the Church.** Ed. Christian Duquoc and Casiano Floristán. 0 8164 2168 4 128pp.
110. **Moral Formation and Christianity.** Ed. Franz Bockle and Jacques Marie Pohier. 0 8164 2169 2 120pp.
111. **Communication in the Church.** Ed. Gregory Baum and Andrew Greeley. 0 8164 2170 6 126pp.
112. **Liturgy and Human Passage.** Ed. David Power and Luis Maldonado. 0 8164 2608 2 136pp.
113. **Revelation and Experience.** Ed. Edward Schillebeeckx and Bas van Iersel. 0 8164 2609 0 134pp.
114. **Evangelization in the World Today.** Ed. Norbert Greinacher and Alois Müller. 0 8164 2610 4 136pp.
115. **Doing Theology in New Places.** Ed. Jean-Pierre Jossua and Johannes Baptist Metz. 0 8164 2611 2 120pp.
116. **Buddhism and Christianity.** Ed. Claude Geffré and Mariasusai Dhavamony. 0 8164 2612 0 136pp.
117. **The Finances of the Church.** Ed. William Bassett and Peter Huizing. 0 8164 2197 8 160pp.
118. **An Ecumenical Confession of Faith?** Ed. Hans Küng and Jürgen Moltmann. 0 8164 2198 6 136pp.
119. **Discernment of the Spirit and of Spirits.** Ed. Casiano Floristán and Christian Duquoc. 0 8164 2199 4 136pp.
120. **The Death Penalty and Torture.** Ed. Franz Bockle and Jacques Marie Pohier. 0 8164 2200 1 136pp.
121. **The Family in Crisis or in Transition.** Ed. Andrew Greely. 0 567 30001 3 128pp.
122. **Structures of Initiation in Crisis.** Ed. Luis Maldonado and David Power. 0 567 30002 1 128pp.
123. **Heaven.** Ed. Bas van Iersel and Edward Schillebeeckx. 0 567 30003 X 120pp.
124. **The Church and the Rights of Man.** Ed. Alois Müller and Norbert Greinacher. 0 567 30004 8 140pp.
125. **Christianity and the Bourgeoisie.** Ed. Johannes Baptist Metz. 0 567 30005 6 144pp.
126. **China as a Challenge to the Church.** Ed. Claude Geffré and Joseph Spae. 0 567 30006 4 136pp.
127. **The Roman Curia and the Communion of Churches.** Ed. Peter Huizing and Knut Walf. 0 567 30007 2 144pp.
128. **Conflicts about the Holy Spirit.** Ed. Hans Küng and Jürgen Moltmann. 0 567 30008 0 144pp.
129. **Models of Holiness.** Ed. Christian Duquoc and Casiano Floristán. 0 567 30009 9 128pp.
130. **The Dignity of the Despised of the Earth.** Ed. Jacques Marie Pohier and Dietmar Mieth. 0 567 30010 2 144pp.
131. **Work and Religion.** Ed. Gregory Baum. 0 567 30011 0 148pp.
132. **Symbol and Art in Worship.** Ed. Luis Maldonado and David Power. 0 567 30012 9 136pp.
133. **Right of the Community to a Priest.** Ed. Edward Schillebeeckx and Johannes Baptist Metz. 0 567 30013 7 148pp.
134. **Women in a Men's Church.** Ed. Virgil Elizondo and Norbert Greinacher. 0 567 30014 5 144pp.
135. **True and False Universality of Christianity.** Ed. Claude Geffré and Jean-Pierre Jossua. 0 567 30015 3 138pp.
136. **What is Religion? An Inquiry for Christian Theology.** Ed. Mircea Eliade and David Tracy. 0 567 30016 1 98pp.
137. **Electing our Own Bishops.** Ed. Peter Huizing and Knut Walf. 0 567 30017 X 112pp.
138. **Conflicting Ways of Interpreting the Bible.** Ed. Hans Küng and Jürgen Moltmann. 0 567 30018 8 112pp.
139. **Christian Obedience.** Ed. Casiano Floristán and Christian Duquoc. 0 567 30019 6 96pp.
140. **Christian Ethics and Economics: the North-South Conflict.** Ed. Dietmar Mieth and Jacques Marie Pohier. 0 567 30020 X 128pp.

1981

141. **Neo-Conservatism: Social and Religious Phenomenon.** Ed. Gregory Baum and John Coleman. 0 567 30021 8.
142. **The Times of Celebration.** Ed. David Power and Mary Collins. 0 567 30022 6.
143. **God as Father.** Ed. Edward Schillebeeckx and Johannes Baptist Metz. 0 567 30023 4.
144. **Tensions Between the Churches of the First World and the Third World.** Ed. Virgil Elizondo and Norbert Greinacher. 0 567 30024 2.
145. **Nietzsche and Christianity.** Ed. Claude Geffré and Jean-Pierre Jossua. 0 567 30025 0.
146. **Where Does the Church Stand?** Ed. Giuseppe Alberigo. 0 567 30026 9.
147. **The Revised Code of Canon Law: a Missed Opportunity?** Ed. Peter Huizing and Knut Walf. 0 567 30027 7.
148. **Who Has the Say in the Church?** Ed. Hans Küng and Jürgen Moltmann. 0 567 30028 5.
149. **Francis of Assisi Today.** Ed. Casiano Floristán and Christian Duquoc. 0 567 30029 3.
150. **Christian Ethics: Uniformity, Universality, Pluralism.** Ed. Jacques Pohier and Dietmar Mieth. 0 567 30030 7.

ll back issues are still in print and available for sale. Orders should be sent to the publishers,

T. & T. CLARK LIMITED

36 George Street, Edinburgh EH2 2LQ, Scotland